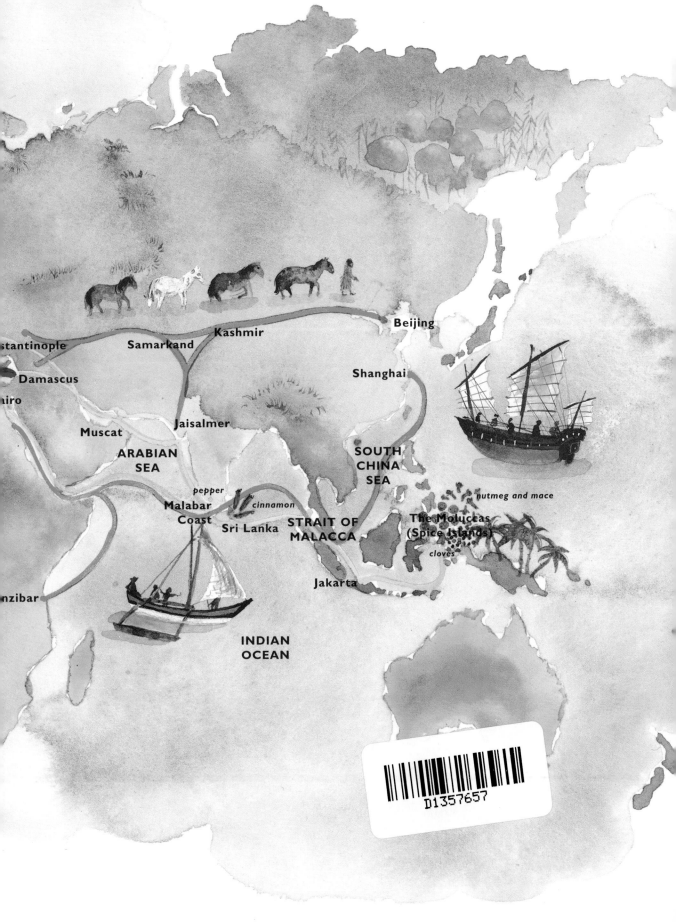

Beijing

stantinople

Damascus

airo

Samarkand

Kashmir

Shanghai

Muscat

Jaisalmer

ARABIAN
SEA

SOUTH
CHINA
SEA

*pepper*

Malabar
Coast

*cinnamon*

Sri Lanka

STRAIT OF
MALACCA

*nutmeg and mace*

The Moluccas
(Spice Islands)

*cloves*

nzibar

Jakarta

INDIAN
OCEAN

# the spice
# routes

# the spice routes

## Chris & Carolyn Caldicott

Recipe photography by James Merrell

FRANCES LINCOLN

Frances Lincoln Limited
4 Torriano Mews
Torrano Avenue
London NW5 2RZ

The Spice Routes
Copyright © Frances Lincoln Limited 2001
Text copyright © Chris and Carolyn Caldicott 2001
Travel photographs © Chris Caldicott
Recipe photographs © James Merrell

First Frances Lincoln edition 2001

British Library Cataloguing-in-Publication data
A catalogue record for this book is available from the British Library

Printed and bound in Singapore

ISBN 0 7112 1756 4

9 8 7 6 5 4 3 2 1

**HALF-TITLE PAGE:** *The clear waters of the Indian Ocean have been the setting for some of the most dramatic events in the history of the spice trade.*

**TITLE PAGE:** *Arab dhows provided maritime transport for the first traders of the Arabian Gulf with the ports on the Malabar Coast of India.*

**ABOVE LEFT:** *A colonial monastery built by the Spanish in the Sacred Valley near Cuzco, Peru.*

**ABOVE RIGHT:** *A boy from Rajasthan, where merchants grew rich on the profits from overland spice routes.*

**RIGHT:** *A stall in the spice souk of the Moroccan port of Essaouira.*

**PAGES 6–7:** *The Malabar Coast of India was for centuries a major centre of the world spice trade.*

# contents

# introduction

The cuisines of the world have been influenced by cultural preferences for different tastes as much as by local climate or geography. Many of the spices used to create the tastes we love originated in just one region of tropical forest or a remote group of islands. International trade in these spices began thousands of years ago. Fortunes have been made and lost in the spice trade. The search for new routes to the sources of valuable seeds, roots, barks and fruits has inspired eras of global discovery and caused large-scale movements of cultures and people around the world.

The diverse communities who have migrated to new lands continue to import their own favourite foods and spices. As a result, even the most exotic ingredients are becoming commonplace in supermarkets the world over. The scope for eclectic cookery in our homes is wider today than it has ever been, as is our awareness of the commodities that are shipped around the world for our pleasure.

In this book we explore the routes spices travelled from sources to markets. Here are historical tales, personal journeys, recipes inspired by the spices, and images of the people and lands of the spice routes.

# the spice trade

The earliest physical evidence of an international spice trade is found in the wall reliefs of the Dayr al-Bahri funerary monument of the pharaonic Queen Hatshepsut built on the west bank of the river Nile at Thebes. They are nearly 3,500 years old.

The reliefs depict journeys via a system of canals and lakes linking the Nile delta with the Red Sea. From here the ancient Egyptians sailed south to a land known as Punt, somewhere in the horn of Africa. The main purpose of these journeys seems to have been to procure resins like frankincense and myrrh for use as perfume and in embalming rituals. However, there is also evidence that cinnamon was used in these ancient burial chambers. As cinnamon is indigenous only to the island of Sri Lanka there was clearly an ancient maritime trade with the Indies across the Arabian Sea. There were probably even earlier overland routes trading pepper from the Indies up the Indus valley and over the Khyber Pass to Mesopotamia and the Levant.

The pharaonic Egyptians were not the only early consumers of spices from Asia. Around 1000 BC, the Phoenicians, from their base of Tyre, in what is now southern Lebanon, were trading spices as far west as southern Spain and even Cornwall and east to the coasts of East Africa and India. Cornwall provided useful metals, while the eastern Mediterranean had plenty of its own spices to trade for the pepper and cinnamon brought from the east. Cumin, coriander, fennel, fenugreek, sesame, dill, caraway, poppy, nigella and anise are all native to the region.

By the time of Alexander the Great in the fourth century BC these were being traded around the shores of the Mediterranean and back along the overland pepper routes with Alexander's armies on their treks eastwards as far as the Indus. The passion for spices among the cooks of ancient Greece was maintained by those of Imperial Rome. By the first century AD, an overland Silk Route to China had been established and both Roman and Arab sailors were exploiting the monsoon trade winds between the ports of the Gulf and the Malabar Coast of India.

Spices were becoming an ever more lucrative trading commodity. The trade was dominated by pepper, a spice that grew only in the tropical forests along the Malabar Coast of south-western India. The principal reason for pepper's high value was that it made salted meat palatable; as salting was for centuries almost the only form of food preservation, demand for pepper was insatiable. To this day, salt and pepper remain ubiquitous and inseparable seasonings. For their part, the cooks of India became enthusiastic for Mediterranean spices as well as for many from

PAGES 8–9: *For centuries, overland spice routes across India, Central Asia, Arabia and North Africa depended almost exclusively on camel caravans.*

LEFT: *The Sphinx at the foot of the pyramids at Giza was carved from a single slab of limestone about four and a half thousand years ago.*

further east. As navigation and shipping skills in the Far East developed, merchant junks travelled west from China, laden with spices such as cassia bark from the hill country near Burma and star anise from the Huang Shan Mountains. Indian, Arab and Chinese traders also collected cloves, nutmeg and mace from the Moluccas in Indonesia, for centuries known simply as the Spice Islands. All these spices were traded for the valuable little dried black corns of pepper and other spices of the Malabar Coast.

*Venice grew to be rich and beautiful on the profits gained from its monopoly of the European spice trade in the fourteenth and fifteenth centuries.*

Malabar ports such as Cochin became the busiest in the world. For the next thousand years, a sea trade with China thrived to the east without middlemen. However, the dhows that sailed westwards across the Arabian Sea to the Gulf and Red Sea ports still needed to transfer their cargoes of pepper and spices to great caravans of camels for the journey to the spice markets in the souks of Cairo, Aleppo and Byzantium. Arab merchants exploited the fall of the Roman Empire to monopolize the east–west trade. Trade around the Mediterranean became dominated by the Moors, and the Islamic Empire spread across North Africa to Spain. The north shore of the Mediterranean was not back in the spice business until the emergence of merchants from the city states of northern Italy.

From the tenth century, Venetian ships had been collecting spices from Levantine and Egyptian ports and distributing them around Europe. But when, in the thirteenth century, the Mameluke sultans in Egypt reconstructed the ancient pharaonic canal system linking Cairo with the Red Sea, and channelled all the spice routes between east and west through it, the opportunity emerged for the two nations to forge a powerful monopoly over the entire European spice trade. Cairo entered a golden period of intellectual, cultural and architectural development.

Prices were forced higher and higher and by the fifteenth century Venice had become rich and beautiful, the envy of the emerging maritime nations of western Europe. The race was on to discover an alternative route to the source of Asian spices. In 1487, the Portuguese navigator Bartholomeu Diaz found a route round the Cape of Good Hope to the Indian Ocean. He was followed in 1497 by Vasco da Gama, who made it all the way to Calicut on the Malabar Coast to begin a trade that would undercut the Venetians and bring great riches to the merchants of Lisbon.

In 1492, Spain dispatched the Genoese navigator Christopher Columbus across the Atlantic to find a faster route to the East Indies. His unexpected arrival in the Americas changed history. The timing of the European awareness of the Americas was significant as it coincided with the isolationist policies of the Ming Dynasty in China. Prior to the Ming, especially during the reign of the Mongol emperor Kublai Khan, China had been a maritime power more sophisticated and successful in the arts of navigation and of foreign trade than any nation in Europe. If China had not abandoned the sort of foreign settlement that had established Chinese communities all over Asia, it seems inevitable that its navigators would eventually have crossed the Pacific and arrived in the Americas before any Europeans.

The Spanish and Portuguese pioneered the early settlement of and trade with the Americas, returning to Europe with a host of previously unknown commodities. In Mexico the Aztecs introduced early conquistadors to chocolate, vanilla, tomatoes, maize and chillies: all previously unknown beyond the shores of America. Further south in the Peruvian Andes, the Incas were also using chillies and maize as well as potatoes, quinine bark as an antimalarial drug and coca as a stimulant. These products have played important roles in world history. Without quinine European ambitions of colonial administration and settlement in the tropics would have been defeated by malaria. Maize has become a staple food of almost all sub-Saharan Africa, the potato a favourite vegetable from County Cork to Kathmandu. Chocolate and vanilla have become essential to the multinational confectionery industry.

On the islands of the Caribbean, Columbus showed the indigenous people the peppercorns he was searching for and they brought him some dried unripe berries of very similar appearance from a local tree. These were not pepper, but what we now know as allspice. In terms of spicing food though, it was the chilli that changed everything. No one in India, Thailand, Malaysia or Indonesia had seen or heard of a chilli until Portuguese ships arrived laden with them in the sixteenth century. The hot cuisine spiced with chillies which we think of as typical of those countries is in fact a relatively modern phenomenon.

The Portuguese spread themselves too thinly, with settlements in Brazil, the Azores, West, South and East Africa, the Gulf, Goa, Cochin, Melaka, Java and Macau. What is more, profits from the spice trade were going straight to private merchants rather than to the Portuguese crown, so the possibility of a cohesive empire was severely limited. The Spanish, despite being the first to find a new route to the Spice Islands by sailing west across the Pacific, also fell into decline economically, as a result of costly naval campaigns against England and France.

The Dutch and British were quick to exploit an opportunity and both set up East India Companies with the aim of dominating world trade. After years of conflict and competition the Dutch secured dominance of the Spice Islands, which produced cloves, nutmeg and mace. The British eventually occupied India, Sri Lanka and the Malay Peninsula, rich in pepper and other spices. Each protected its monopoly by forbidding the transportation of any seeds of the spices they controlled.

These monopolies were eventually broken by the French when the appropriately named Pierre Poivre successfully pilfered and replanted

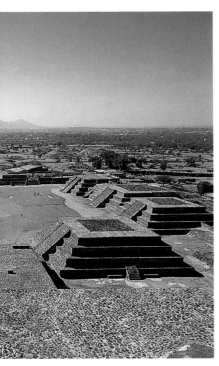

spices from the Indies on the French colony of Mauritius in the Indian Ocean. The French soon had plantations on all their Indian Ocean islands, although they were to lose most of these to the British as spoils of war after the defeat of Napoleon at Waterloo.

On the other side of the world the British, French and Dutch occupied most of the islands of the Caribbean and the Guyanas on the north coast of South America. All of these became hosts to plantations not just of spices but of products such as sugar and bananas. To work these plantations, millions of Africans were forcibly resettled as slaves. The rest of South America remained dominated either by the Spanish or the Portuguese and their African slaves. The indigenous cooking traditions from southern Europe and Africa mixed with those of the descendants of the Incas, Mayans and Aztecs.

Surprisingly, Africa has not produced a single spice that has been important in the spice trade. However, large numbers of exotic spcies were introduced into Africa by European traders wh established African ports as convenient stopping places. As a result, African cuisine uses some of the most complex and varied mixtures of spices anywhere in the world. The most enthusiastic importers of spices have been the coastal countries of West Africa.

Many of the lands that were once colonized by European powers have developed their own thiving spice production industries. Sri Lanka has held on to its position as the world's largest supplier of cinnamon, Grenada refers to itself as the Spice Island of the Caribbean and is a major exporter of nutmeg, and Zanzibar now sends cloves around the world.

The impact northern America and Australia have had on the global trade in spices has been as emerging markets rather than as suppliers. The United States in particular has become the largest market in the world in the modern spice trade, which has contributed to the immense wealth of some of its cities. The great diversity of peoples from all over the world who have settled in the West has contributed to ever-evolving eclectic mixtures of cuisines and of the spices required to create them.

**ABOVE LEFT:** *A road through the Huang Shan Mountains of southwest China, the source of star anise.*

**LEFT:** *Ruins of the once mighty architecture of Teotihuacán, the largest of Mexico's pre-Hispanic empires.*

# what are spices?

The word 'spice' and its equivalents in other Romance languages derive from the Latin word *species*, which originally referred to merchandise, particularly from the east. For thousands of years, spices have been among the most valuable commodities traded worldwide, but defining what they are is not easy. The commodities that are commonly thought of as spices today comprise seeds, berries, flowers, fruits, kernels, roots, rhizomes, leaves, arils, barks and saps that are used in cooking and food preparation. Their common feature is their aromatic qualities that throughout history have been used individually or in combination to flavour food and to make eating more enjoyable.

While no spices are eaten on their own, most have significant nutritional value, and many have also been used as cures and medicines. These properties have added to their perceived and real value in lands distant from their origin. Some spices which will only grow in tropical conditions have found large markets in far-off temperate countries, being transported there in dried form. Other plants have been grown successfully in foreign countries, thus providing fresh produce to new consumers. Yet others have just not been traded far from their lands of origin. For example, capers and sumac have never found much use in cooking beyond the Mediterranean; ajwain seeds, amchoor, kokum, kal nemak and zedoary are still only used in Indian recipes; Sichuan pepper is only rarely used in non-Chinese dishes, or melegueta pepper beyond West Africa.

The most sought-after and valuable spices traded along overland and sea routes are: saffron (the stigmas of the crocus flower); the berries of pepper and allspice; the seeds of cumin, coriander, fennel, fenugreek, mustard, nigella, sesame and anise; the fruits of cardamom, capsicum (including chilli, cayenne and paprika), tamarind, vanilla and star anise; the rhizomes of ginger, galangal and turmeric; the bark of cinnamon and cassia; the flowers of clove; the kernel of nutmeg and its aril mace; and the leaves of lemon grass, kari patta (curry leaves), coriander, fenugreek and makrut lime.

# the use of spices

All the spices in this book are available in the West, and although a few of them may require a trip to a specialist food store in a city where there is an appropriate ethnic community, most should be found easily in regular supermarkets or delicatessens. Most fresh spices – such as galangal, lemon grass, curry and lime leaves – can be bought in quantity and frozen at home for future use.

Spices need looking after. All dry spices should be kept in airtight containers in the dark and wet spice mixtures sealed and refrigerated. They all keep better in whole rather than ground form, so grinding should be carried out only as needed. Some people prefer the ritual and satisfaction of grinding spices by hand with a pestle and mortar, others the convenience of an electric grinder.

Most spices must be heated to release their flavour and become palatable, and this is often done at the start of the recipe, by frying them in oil or by dry-roasting. Occasionally, the dish's flavour needs to be tempered by adding the spices just before serving.

One of the most frequent questions we are asked in the World Food Café is 'How spicy is it?' What people usually mean by this is 'How much chilli is in it?' Dishes can be laced with wonderful combinations of aromatic spices without being particularly 'hot'. On the other hand, just one spice as hot as a 'Scotch bonnet' or 'Habanero' chilli can turn a meal into a mind- and body-altering experience. There is a lot of variation between different people's taste for and tolerance of spices. For some, the extreme effects of very hot food can be a great pleasure; for others they are an excruciating pain. Most of the recipes in this book are more concerned with the pleasure of combining the subtle tastes of spices to make eating interesting and varied. There are only a couple that will appeal solely to those with masochistic tendencies. Where this is the case it is clearly indicated.

*The busy spice souk in the Medina of Marrakech. Traditional spice mixtures such as harissa and chermoula commonly feature in Moroccan recipes.*

# the eastern
# mediterranean

PAGES 18–19: *The edge of Siwa Oasis in Egypt. Lying 18m/60ft below sea level, this depression provides numerous pools of sweet water which irrigate groves of date palms, olive trees and lemon trees. The oasis was once an important stopover for camel caravans crossing the desert.*

ABOVE: *A temple guard at the Dayr al-Bahri funerary monument of Queen Hatshepsut.*

OPPOSITE: *One of the enormous pillared halls at the Temple of Madinat Habu, built by Rameses III.*

The rocky coasts, desert-fringed hinterlands, woody hillsides and open meadows of the eastern Mediterranean are home to some of the most important spices and herbs in the history of the trade. Cumin, coriander, fennel, fenugreek, sesame, nigella, anise, poppy, caraway, capers, thyme, parsley, mint and oregano all originated in the area which today covers Egypt, the countries of the Levant, Turkey, Greece, the Balkans and southern Italy. As a result of prolific trading along the spice routes, however, many of these have become associated more with their countries of adoption than with their lands of origin.

As long ago as 3500 BC, the ancient Egyptians were using local spices to flavour their food, in cosmetics and in lotions for embalming their dead. The Egyptians liked to cook their meat slowly, infusing their dishes with herbs and spices. While most of those used, including cumin, coriander, fennel, anise and poppy seed, would have been plentiful locally, there is evidence that by the second millennium BC other spices were already being brought from overseas. On the walls of Dayr al-Bahri, the funerary monument of the only woman to proclaim herself Pharaoh, Queen Hatshepsut (*c.* 1512–1482 BC), a series of reliefs depicts journeys by boat to the land of Punt to collect frankincense, myrrh and other spices. Nothing remains of Punt, which is assumed to have been somewhere in Somalia or Ethiopia on the shores of the Red Sea, but whoever the people of Punt were, they appear to have been among the first to trade spices over long distances.

By the time of Rameses II (*c.* 1304–1237 BC), Egyptian ships were sailing into the Persian Gulf as far as the Euphrates and what was then Mesopotamia, and Egypt became a lucrative market for spices from further and further afield. New overland routes across the River Indus, through the Khyber Pass, across Afghanistan and Persia to Babylon, brought spices such as pepper, ginger, cardamom, turmeric and cinnamon from the Malabar Coast of India and from Ceylon (now Sri Lanka).

The ancient Greeks, in contrast, stuck largely to Mediterranean herbs, and showed little interest in spices from the East, with the exception of cinnamon and saffron. But with the conquests of Alexander the Great (356–323 BC) the patterns of the ancient world changed. Alexander ruled over an empire that stretched from Egypt to the Indus, and goods, including spices, were traded along protected routes not only between east and west but all around the Mediterranean.

By the first century BC Rome was at the centre of Mediterranean power. The Romans extended their empire and their trading routes as far

as the Arabian Gulf and the Caspian Sea. They even embarked on their own sea voyages to India. In the first century AD, the Roman nobleman Apicius wrote a book of recipes in Latin which has survived to illustrate the Roman enthusiasm for pepper, cloves, cardamom and ginger, as well as cumin, coriander and caraway.

During the turbulent centuries between the fall of Rome in the fifth century AD and the rise of the Italian city states, spice trading across much of the Mediterranean was reduced to little more than the sale of booty acquired by pirates, bandits and returning crusaders. Further east, however, Arab merchants developed a trade in spices as far as the Malabar Coast of India, Ceylon, the Spice Islands of Indonesia and even China. Nutmeg, mace, cloves and cassia bark joined pepper, turmeric, ginger, cardamom and cinnamon as common and valuable commodities.

In 1295 Marco Polo returned to Venice from his journeys in China and India with knowledge and contacts that would give it the essential edge over its Italian rivals. Meanwhile, the Mamelukes – the military clan of Turkish ex-slaves who ruled Egypt from the mid-thirteenth century – had stabilized the eastern shores of the Mediterranean. Everything was in place for a flourishing trade. Fleets of Venetian oar- and sail-powered cargo ships, built in the shipyards of the *arsenale*, loaded up valuable cargoes of spices supplied by Arab traders through Cairo and the ports of the Levant. From Venice, merchants distributed these spices to the rest of Europe, making their fortunes in the process.

The emerging maritime nations at the western end of the Mediterranean soon began to look for opportunities to develop their own spice trades. Portugal sent sailors south in search of a route to the Indian Ocean around the coast of Africa. The Spanish, seeking a western route to the Indies, in 1492 arrived instead in the Americas. Before long, Lisbon had eclipsed Venice as the most important city for spice trading in Europe, and the Spanish were delivering exciting new spices and foods from the Americas.

*During the height of Venetian dominance of the spice trade in Europe, even small ports like Riomaggiore on the Ligurian coast of Italy received shipments of spices such as pepper all the way from the Malabar Coast of India.*

# aswan

**Saffron**
**(*Crocus sativus*)**

Native to Persia, saffron was among the earliest spices brought to the eastern Mediterranean by Arab traders, and it soon became much sought after. Greece is still a major producer. The Moors took it all the way to Morocco and Spain, where it is still grown and common in popular dishes such as tajines and paellas. The Mughals took it east to India; Kashmir remains one of the principal growers. From here its use spread via Tibet into China.

It is possible that saffron was introduced to northern Europe by Phoenician tin traders travelling to Cornwall many centuries before Christ, but attempts at commercial production were inspired by returning crusaders who brought back corms from Asia Minor between the fourteenth and sixteenth centuries. In England, the cultivation of saffron became so well established around the Essex town of Walden that it changed its name to Saffron Walden. Saffron-growing spread through Italy and France too.

Because it is necessary to harvest by hand the stigmas of the crocus flowers that produce the spice, and a huge number of flowers is needed to supply even a kilo, saffron remains the most costly spice in the world. The most common use of saffron is to add colour and subtle flavour to rice dishes such as Indian biryani, Iranian pilaf and Milanese risotto.

**Felucca *sailing boats on the***
***river Nile.***

The spice merchants in Aswan's glittering souk put a wonderfully creative effort into the visual splendour of their stalls, pandering to every fantasy a tourist might have of a spice market in an Arab bazaar. By day the illusion is compromised by the harsh desert sun and the heat, dust and flies that come with it. Nightfall relieves some of the heat. Darkness is kept at bay by a festival of lights as bright and gaudy as a fairground, and the labyrinth of lanes and alleyways running along the east bank of the Nile is full of life. The picture is complete with turbaned men in dusty hooded cloaks (*jallabas*) masked women swathed in black and gold, donkey carts fighting their way through the crowds laden with oranges, tomatoes and bunches of coriander, the shouts of the merchants, the banter of bargainers, the wail of Arab music, clouds of incense and whafts of scented smoke from bubbling water pipes.

Saffron, the most valuable spice, is the one the Aswan merchants are most eager to sell. They know the tourists know it's expensive, but they also know most of them can't tell saffron from safflower. Saffron does not grow in the desert climate of Egypt, but thrives in the cooler mountain valleys of Persia, Kashmir, Spain and Morocco. Safflower is a thistle used as a vegetable dye that grows with abundance around Aswan and is of miniscule value compared to saffron. The spice sellers play a clever game. Well aware that tourists may be suspicious of their trade, their first attempt to sell saffron is to offer a scoop from a seductive mound of bright yellow Indian turmeric powder. Anyone taking issue with this offer is congratulated on their culinary experience. The turmeric mound is dismissed as inferior 'Sudanese saffron', and a theatrical display of pride accompanies the presentation of a few stigmas of safflower safely stapled up in a plastic bag. The impossibly low price demanded for this bag, the equivalent to about one English pound, immediately confirms the bogus nature of its contents. 'This is only Egyptian saffron, that is why it is cheap', is the well-rehearsed reaction to this observation. 'You want best quality Persian saffron?' From a small tin hidden under the counter comes a much smaller plastic bag with a few dark orange twigs inside, but incredibly, this also costs only one pound. We buy it anyway and take it back to the cook on our boat to see if he can tell us what it is. He immediately recognizes it as ossfor: a near-worthless pickling herb.

## EGYPTIAN LENTIL SOUP

*We had sailed to Aswan from Luxor on a boat called the* Oberoi Philae. *The cooks on board came up with some above-average versions of the Egyptian staples and several dishes that were new to us. Of all the dishes on offer, however, our favourites were the Egyptian lentil soup and the bean purée.*

SERVES 4

**For the soup**

175g/6oz red split lentils
2 teaspoons cumin seeds
4 tablespoons olive oil
1 large onion, chopped
2 garlic cloves, chopped
1 medium potato, peeled and cubed
2 leeks, washed and sliced
2 beetroots, peeled and cubed

575ml/1pt chicken stock
juice of 1 lemon
salt and ground black pepper

**For the garnish**

3 tablespoons olive oil
4 garlic cloves, chopped
1 teaspoon cumin seeds
handful of flat-leaf parsley, chopped

Rinse the lentils until the water runs clear. Dry-roast the cumin seeds for both the soup and the garnish in a small pan until they are aromatic, then grind them to a powder.

In a large saucepan, heat 4 tablespoons of olive oil. Add the onion and the garlic. Fry them until soft, then stir in 2 teaspoons of ground cumin.

Now add the potatoes, leeks and beetroots, stir well and cover the pan. Sweat the vegetables on a low heat until they start to soften. Add the red lentils, the stock and enough water to cover the vegetables well.

Bring to the boil, cover the pan and reduce the heat. Simmer until the lentils are soft and begin to break down, adding water as necessary (lentils soak up a lot of water during cooking). Scoop off any foam and discard it.

Blend the soup in a food processor until smooth, stir in the lemon juice and add salt and pepper to taste.

To make the garnish, heat 3 tablespoons of olive oil in a small pan, and fry 4 garlic cloves until light brown. Add the rest of the ground cumin and fry for a further few seconds. Pour a little on to the surface of each serving of soup and top with chopped parsley.

**Cumin**
**(*Cuminum cyminum*)**
Native to Upper Egypt and the eastern Mediterranean, cumin is a spice from antiquity, found in the tombs of the Pharaohs and used in the cooking of Classical Greece and Rome. There are biblical references to cumin being threshed with a rod in a style still seen in Egypt today. From early times cumin was traded west by the Phoenicians around the Mediterranean and east by the Arabs through Persia and on to India.

The ground powder of dry-roasted cumin seeds has a strong, rather bitter taste, and is still an essential ingredient in the Egyptian condiment *duqqa*. In the Levant it is mixed with walnuts and pomegranate juice as a dipping sauce, in Persia it is a component of *advieh*, in Afghanistan of char masala and in India of garam masala. In India the seeds are also fried whole at the beginning of a recipe or added whole after dry-roasting (which brings out a nutty flavour), to dhal and to yoghurt sauces. In Morocco, as in India, ground cumin is often mixed with the sweeter powder of ground coriander; this is the case with both harissa and ras el hanout. By the sixteenth century cumin was being traded across the Atlantic to the Americas and it is a common ingredient in Mexican recipes such as mole sauces and chilli con carne.

## Sesame
### (Sesamum indicum)

The word sesame can be traced back through the Arabic *simsim* to the ancient Egyptian *semsemt*, an indication of how long this seed has been known and used. The way the pods split open when ripe to release the sought-after seeds is said to have given rise to the phrase 'open sesame', made famous by the story of Ali Baba and the Forty Thieves in *The Arabian Nights*. The spice routes of the early Arab trade with the East took sesame to Persia, to China, and eventually to Japan, where sesame oil is still highly esteemed and the seeds are used widely in both savoury and sweet recipes. Sesame also spread through Africa from east to west, before finding its way on to the ships of slave traders across the Atlantic to the Americas.

Today Guatemala, Mexico and the southern States of the USA are the major producers. However, sesame is still used most extensively and inventively in the area of its origin.

Creamed sesame, known as *tahina*, is a staple of the eastern Mediterranean, eaten on its own or blended with chickpeas in houmous, aubergine and garlic in *baba ghanoush*, lemon juice in tarato and syrups, vanilla and pistachio nuts in halva.

## EGYPTIAN BEAN PURÉE

SERVES 4

### For the purée
1 dessertspoon cumin seeds
4 tablespoons olive oil
1 red onion, chopped
4 garlic cloves, crushed
2 medium leeks, washed and sliced
150g/5oz dried fava beans or broad
 beans, soaked in water overnight
juice of a lemon

handful of flat-leaf parsley, chopped
handful of coriander leaves, chopped
salt and ground black pepper

### For the garnish
2 tablespoons olive oil
5 spring onions, finely sliced
1 dessertspoon sesame seeds
handful of fresh dill, chopped

Dry-roast the cumin seeds until they are aromatic, grind to a powder and set to one side.

In a large saucepan, heat 4 tablespoons of oil and fry the onion, garlic and leeks until soft. Add the ground cumin and the drained fava beans, and stir well. Add enough water to just cover the beans, bring it to the boil, reduce the heat and simmer with a lid on until the beans become very soft.

Blend the beans with the lemon juice in a food processor until smooth. Stir in the chopped parsley, coriander, and salt and pepper to taste, then scoop the mixture into a bowl.

To make the garnish, heat 2 tablespoons of olive oil in a small pan, add the spring onions and sesame seeds and fry until golden. Pile on top of the bean purée. Sprinkle with dill and some additional olive oil. Serve with unleavened bread, such as pitta, and seasoned feta cheese.

## SEASONED FETA CHEESE

MAKES 200G/7OZ

200g/7oz block of feta cheese
1 teaspoon cumin and coriander
 seeds, mixed together, dry-roasted
 until aromatic and ground to a
 powder

1 teaspoon paprika
1 teaspoon ground black pepper
olive oil
handful of flat-leaf parsley, chopped

Cut the cheese into three equal parts. Cover one of these in the cumin and coriander, one in the paprika and one in the black pepper. Sprinkle the cheese with olive oil and chopped parsley. Serve with olives, cubes of cucumber, tomatoes, fresh mint and red onion.

# cairo

During the fourteenth and fifteenth centuries, Cairo grew to be the most important centre of spice trade in the eastern Mediterranean. The Mamelukes, who had seized power in the city in 1254, rebuilt the ancient pharaonic canal system that linked the Nile to the Red Sea. Control of the canals enabled the Mameluke sultans, in partnership with Venetian merchants, to operate a monopoly on the supply of spices between the

Mediterranean and the Indies in both directions. Cairo, like Venice, grew rich from the trade that attracted merchants from distant lands and filled the city with bazaars of exotic spices. It was on these profits that the Mamelukes built most of the beautiful mosques and souk gateways that are seen in Cairo today.

The souks of Cairo, including the huge labyrinth of Khan el-Khalili, still have bustling spice markets. Here, all the influences of Egypt's trading heyday are in evidence. Sacks of seeds, barks, roots and nuts from the East are sold alongside saffron from Persia, filo pastries filled with sweetmeats from Turkey, dried hibiscus, cumin and coriander from the Nile Valley, as well as jars of spicy pastes and sauces containing chillies from across the Atlantic.

The souks provide oases of peace in the form of shabby coffee bars where no one hurries the drinkers of miniature cups of strong black coffee sweetened to a syrup and scented with cardamom, as they puff away at bubbling *shesha* water pipes of molasses-coated tobacco, a legacy from Ottoman times. Hole-in-the-wall takeaways provide fast food snacks of fresh fried felafel in pitta bread with pickled turnip, coloured pink by beetroot and creamy *tahina* dressing. *Duqqa* (Arabic for 'to pound') is an ancient mixture of spices used as a condiment in Egyptian kitchens. It combines dry-roasted cumin, coriander, sesame and nigella seeds with salt, pepper, nuts and mint all pounded to a paste, and is still sold in takeaway paper cones in the spice souks of Cairo.

**PAGES 28–29:** *The great mosques built by the Mamelukes dominate the skyline of modern Cairo.*

**BELOW:** *The spice souk in Cairo's Khan el-Khalili bazaar.*

**Nigella**
**(*Nigella sativa*)**

A spice indigenous to the Levant, nigella is known as *habbet el beraka* or 'seeds of grace', in Egypt. It is commonly used sprinkled on bread, a trend that is prevalent all the way through the Middle East to northern India. India is now the main producer of the spice, and it is especially popular in the eastern state of Bengal where it is one of the five spices in *panch phoron*. Elsewhere in India it is sprinkled on naan bread, or used to flavour pickles, dhal and vegetable dishes.

## MARINATED SEA BASS

*In one of the smarter restaurants of Khan el-Khalili, we enjoyed this marinated sea bass in a sauce flavoured with garlic and spices. It looks complicated, but it is really quite easy and well worth the effort.*

SERVES 4

4 200g/7oz fillets of sea bass
olive oil
plain unbleached flour

### For the marinade
4 tablespoons olive oil
juice of a lemon
3 garlic cloves, chopped
1 tablespoon white wine vinegar
salt and black pepper

### For the sauce
4 tablespoons olive oil
1 large onion, finely sliced
3 garlic cloves, chopped

1/4 teaspoon cloves
1 dessertspoon coriander seeds
1 teaspoon cumin seeds
1 teaspoon fennel seeds
1/2 teaspoon grated nutmeg
1 tablespoon tomato purée
1 teaspoon honey
2 bay leaves
1 teaspoon dried oregano
1 teaspoon dried thyme
450g/1lb plum tomatoes, pulped in a
  food processor
salt and ground black pepper
chopped parsley

Combine the marinade ingredients, pour over the fillets, and set them aside for 1 hour. Meanwhile, make the tomato sauce:

Heat the olive oil in a saucepan and fry the onion and garlic until soft. Dry-roast the cloves, coriander, cumin and fennel seeds until they are aromatic, then grind to a powder. Add to the onion and garlic, along with the grated nutmeg, and stir well.

Add the tomato purée, honey, bay leaves, oregano, thyme and pulped tomato; bring to the boil, reduce the heat, cover the pan and gently simmer until the oil returns.

Remove the fish from the marinade, and pour any remaining liquid into the tomato sauce. Season with salt, black pepper and chopped parsley to taste. Very gently simmer the sauce while you coat the sea bass fillets in unbleached flour and fry them until they are golden brown.

Place the fish on top of the tomato sauce and serve immediately with rice cooked with a pinch of saffron.

# turkey

Any history of Turkish food and its use of spices has to take into account the fact that the Turks did not always live in Turkey. The area covered by modern Turkey was part of Greek, Roman and Byzantine empires long before any Turks arrived in the region. Until the tenth century, the local cuisine presumably resembled that of the rest of the Mediterranean, and would have included the spices arriving in the markets of the Greek city of Byzantium, via both overland caravan routes and Red Sea dhow connections with the Levant.

The Turks were once a nomadic people living in the Central Asian marshes around Xinjiang (now part of China). Their diet seems basically to have consisted of mares' milk, horse meat and unleavened bread (as, indeed, does that of the tribes still living there today). As they moved west towards the end of the first millennium AD, they came into contact with the sophisticated culture of Islamic Persia. They were enthusiastic converts to Islam and borrowed from the Persian language, culture and cuisine.

From the fourteenth century the Turks were ruled by Ottoman sultans. At the height of its power, in the seventeenth century, the Ottoman Empire covered Asia Minor (modern Turkey), Egypt and much of the coast of North Africa, Greece, the Balkans and even Hungary. In the kitchens of the Ottoman sultans' Topkapi Palace in Constantinople, Turkish cookery was elevated to new heights of sophistication, and spices were used with subtlety and imagination.

The Misir Carsisi, or Spice Bazaar, still thrives in Istanbul. The entrance, through armoured doors off Eminonu Square, reveals a scene lit by a combination of dim daylight from high windows in the arched, vaulted ceiling and brash displays of electric light at individual stalls, piled high with *baharat* (spices): many familiar, some from afar and others only to be guessed at. There is an increasing infiltration of tourist shops into the bazaar but not on the scale of Istanbul's other great market, the Grand Bazaar, where merchants are much more likely to be dealers in the goods of Levi and Sony than anything Turkish.

*The ruins of the ancient Syrian city of Hierapolis overlooking Pamukkale, near the Aegean coast of Turkey.*

## TURKISH PILAF

*This is a Turkish pilaf that we ate on a trip south from Istanbul at Pamukkale, a tiny village deep in beautiful Turkish countryside. Tourists are attracted there by the extraordinary snow-white travertine formations over which warm spring water cascades down the hillside.*

Serves 4–6

150g/5oz dried green lentils, soaked in water overnight
150g/5oz cracked bulghur wheat
60g/2oz currants
2 heaped teaspoons coriander seeds
1/2 teaspoon cloves
1/2 teaspoon ground cinnamon
1/2 teaspoon ground cardamom
salt and ground black pepper
2 tablespoons olive oil
60g/2oz pine nuts
3 skinless chicken breasts, cut into thin strips and seasoned with salt and pepper

60g/2oz butter
3 medium carrots, diced
1 large red onion, chopped
150ml/5fl oz chicken stock
2 handfuls of flat-leaf parsley, chopped
handful of coriander leaves, chopped

### For the garnish
575ml/1pt yoghurt
handful of fresh mint leaves, chopped
salt and ground black pepper

Drain the lentils, cover them with water in a saucepan, bring to the boil and simmer until soft.

Meanwhile, place the bulghur and currants in a bowl and just cover them with boiling water. Set to one side for about 10 minutes to allow the bulghur to absorb the water.

Dry-roast the coriander seeds and cloves until aromatic, then grind to a powder. Combine them with the remaining spices and set to one side.

In a wok, heat the olive oil and add the pine nuts, turning frequently. When golden, remove them from the wok and set to one side. Fry the chicken strips in the wok until golden brown.

Add the butter, and when it has melted add the carrots and onion and fry them until soft. Add the spice mixture, the drained cooked lentils, then the bulghur wheat, the currants and the stock. Stir well, cover the wok, reduce the heat and gently steam for 5 minutes.

Finally, add the flat-leaf parsley. Turn out on a large dish, and sprinkle with coriander and pine nuts. Serve immediately with yoghurt mixed with chopped fresh mint, salt and pepper, and a crunchy green salad.

*Turkish pilaf*

# pelion

The mountainous peninsula of Pelion stretches out into the Aegean Sea, almost encircling the tranquil Pagasitic Gulf. The sheltered port of the gulf, Vólos, has seen a thriving trade since antiquity. It was from here that Jason and the Argonauts set sail in their quest for the Golden Fleece. Mount Pelion was the summer home of the Olympian gods. Until recently there were no roads on the peninsula, and the villages are still linked by paved paths shaded by forests of chestnut, apple, beech and plane trees. The lack of roads and the mountainous terrain helped Pelion to remain relatively autonomous during Ottoman occupation, allowing local merchants to continue trade with Alexandria and Cairo in preference to Istanbul, until Egypt too fell into Ottoman hands.

Pelion cuisine offers some pleasant variations of Greek favourites. One memorable lunch we had there began with a local hooch called *tipouro*: an earthy and robust version of the normally fresh-tasting ouzo, served in miniature plain glass bottles and accompanied by small bowls of a pickled mountain herb called *tsitsiravla*. A feast ensued. Bowls of bean soup made with carrots, celery and herbs and eaten with fresh-baked cheese bread were followed by deep-fried cheese and potato cakes served with a coleslaw of shredded carrot, cabbage and peppers with garlic, chilli and parsley, all soaked in olive oil. The main course was *spetzofai*, a dish of spiced sausage, aubergine and peppers in a tomato sauce. We were to taste many variations of this during our visit.

In Agios Georgios we stayed in the antique opulence of the recently restored villa of a nineteenth-century merchant. Arhontiko Ioannidi, like many of his fellow Pelian merchants, made his fortune in Egypt by shipping the apples, olives, beans and chestnuts that are abundant on the slopes of the mountain across the sea to Alexandria. The ceilings in his mansion were painted by local artists, with references to both Egyptian and Greek mythology, including a portrait of Hermes, the god of trade. The Egyptian connections of merchants like Ioannidi may explain the use of Asian spices such as cinnamon, nutmeg and cloves in the traditional family recipes for spiced olive oils, vinegars and preserves.

In the hills above Vólos, we found more thriving herb- and spice-related cottage industries. The narrow paved streets of Makrinítsa are lined with stalls selling packets of herbs, spices and flower petals, and jars of

## Coriander
### (*Coriandrum sativum*)

Native to the shores of the eastern Mediterranean and to the Middle East, coriander has had medical and culinary uses since ancient Egyptian times. The Greeks used it to flavour wine and Roman legionaries carried it to flavour bread. Like cumin, coriander found its way as far west as Morocco with Phoenician traders and east all the way to India on the earliest spice routes.

Coriander leaves remain so popular in Middle Eastern cookery they are often referred to as Arab parsley. The seeds, leaves and roots of coriander are all used in cooking. The seeds, which have a sweet slightly citrus flavour, are ground and used in spice mixtures in Europe and North Africa, while across the whole of Asia, it is the leaves that are popular. In India ground coriander is an essential component of garam masala, the seeds being used whole, fried at the beginning of cooking, and the pulped root is used to thicken stews and curries, as it also is in Thailand. Across the Atlantic, coriander leaves are popular all over the American continent.

preserved chestnuts and figs, and lead to a village square and several taver-nas suspended above a panoramic view of the city. We ate a particularly good version of *spetzofai* here and some delicious *melitzana*, which is a smoky aubergine, garlic and olive oil purée. Even the Greek salad was exceptionally fine, with feta marinated in herbs, succulent Vólos olives, sweet red onion, and cucumbers, sweet peppers and tomatoes speckled with fresh dill. Throughout the meal a dramatic electrical storm raged over Vólos and the normally tranquil gulf.

**RIGHT:** *Basil growing on a Pelion windowsill.*

**BELOW:** *The clear waters of the Pagasitic Gulf.*

## PELION SPETZOFAI

*The Spanish* chorizo, *which is easy to find in supermarkets, makes a good substitute for the spicy sausage used in the original version of the recipe.*

SERVES 4

6 tablespoons olive oil
4 garlic cloves, chopped
I large red onion, finely sliced
2 red peppers, sliced
2 small aubergines, cubed
salt to taste
2 teaspoons paprika
2 dessertspoons fennel seeds

I teaspoon dried oregano
2 red chillies, chopped
175g/6oz sliced spicy *chorizo* sausage,
    cut into quarters
400g/14oz plum tomatoes, pulped in
    a food processor
I tablespoon tomato purée

Heat the oil in a large saucepan. Fry the garlic, onion and peppers until they start to soften. Add the aubergine and sprinkle with a little salt. Continue frying until all the vegetables are soft, then add the paprika, fennel seeds, oregano, chillies and spicy sausage.

Stir well and mix in the pulped plum tomatoes and the tomato purée. Add a little water to make a sauce. Bring to the boil, then reduce the heat, cover the pan and simmer gently until the sauce looks reduced and rich.

Serve with a Greek salad (see below) and crusty bread.

## PELION-STYLE GREEK SALAD

SERVES 4

¹/₂ small cos lettuce, finely sliced
handful of chopped dill
2 medium carrots, grated
I red pepper, finely sliced
¹/₄ small red cabbage, finely sliced
2 handfuls of flat-leaf parsley
handful of fresh mint leaves, chopped
225g/8oz feta cheese
150g/5oz black olives

**For the dressing**

6 tablespoons olive oil
2 garlic cloves, crushed
2 red chillies, finely chopped
juice of 2 lemons
I teaspoon dried oregano
salt and black pepper to taste

Mix the cos lettuce and the dill in a salad bowl. Combine the grated carrot, pepper, cabbage, parsley and mint and pile the mixture over the lettuce. Add feta cheese and olives. Mix the dressing ingredients and pour on top.

*Pelion-style Greek salad*

# corfu

The Ionian islands off the west coast of Greece made convenient stopping places for the Venetian merchant fleet as it brought cargoes of eastern spices from the ports of Egypt and the Levant back to northern Italy. Legacies of this Venetian past are the olive groves that so dominate rural vistas on the islands, as well as the elegant town of Kérkyra, capital of Corfu. Every morning in the shadow of the fortress (which still shows the stone-carved emblem of Venice) there is an open-air market selling scoops of spices, fresh herbs, wild strawberries, mounds of olives and local delicacies such as courgette flowers.

In Strinilas we stopped for lunch in a café in the village square. We were served a *meze* that included chargrilled aubergines and pickled chillies: a far cry from the lukewarm moussakas of tourist legend. Even more interesting was the meal we had in Kérkyra: this red mullet flavoured with a buttery fennel, fenugreek and garlic stuffing.

## WHOLE RED MULLET WITH FENNEL AND FENUGREEK

SERVES 4

2 tablespoons fenugreek seeds
60g/2oz butter
2 garlic cloves, crushed
1 large red onion, sliced
3 bulbs of fennel, finely sliced
salt and ground black pepper

4 300g/10oz red mullet, scaled and
  gutted (you can ask your fishmonger
  to do this)
3 tablespoons olive oil
juice of 2 lemons

Pre-heat the oven to 180°C/350°F/gas 4.

Dry-roast the fenugreek seeds until aromatic and grind to a powder.

In a frying pan, gently melt the butter and fry the garlic, onion and fennel until they start to soften. Add the fenugreek and season with salt and pepper. Stir well and remove from the heat.

Place the mullet in a large baking tray, and place some fennel mixture inside the cavity of each fish. Sprinkle olive oil and lemon juice over the top and season with salt and pepper. Cover with foil and bake for 15 minutes, then remove the foil and bake for a further 15 minutes.

Serve with boiled new potatoes covered with butter and fresh mint.

**Fenugreek
(*Trigonella foenum-graecum*)**
As a spice native to both the eastern Mediterranean and Asia, fenugreek has not needed to travel between these two regions. The Greeks used to grow fenugreek as cattle fodder (it became known as 'Greek hay'); they still use the seeds in fish dishes.

In India the seeds are either fried in hot oil at the begining of cooking or dry-roasted and ground to a powder and added to spice mixtures. As they are very rich in protein, minerals and vitamins, fenugreek seeds are especially valuable in poorer rural communities where diet may be limited. The young leaves of fenugreek are popular in northern India and Pakistan, where they are known as *meti* and used to flavour meat, chicken, vegetable and fried cheese dishes. In Ethiopia fenugreek is an ingredient of the blend of spices known as *berbere*.

*Whole red mullet with fennel
and fenugreek*

# pantelleria

When the wind blows warm from Africa, the temporarily resident glitterati of Pantelleria panic a little. The *scirocco* builds up in the empty furnace of the Sahara, rushes north, then rolls, hot and dry, over the Mediterranean. The first land to challenge it is Pantelleria, a desert island in sight of Tunisia, but owned by the more distant Italy.

Pantelleria was on the Phoenician trade routes around the Mediterranean over a thousand years before Christ. The Moors, who occupied the island between the tenth and fourteenth centuries AD, named it Bent el-Rhia, which means 'daughter of the winds'. But the *scirocco*, like the gusting *mistral* in the south of France and the dusty *libeccio* of Algeria, is only an occasional visitor. For most of the year Pantelleria is warm, dry and sunny; good weather and bad are determined purely by the winds. On good days, and there are plenty of them, Pantelleria, with its crystal-clear sea, intriguing Moorish architecture and dramatic volcanic, mountainous interior is one of the most delightfully exotic destinations in Europe. On bad days people stay indoors. During our stay we were regularly fed warnings of a threateningly imminent *scirocco*, particularly from anyone who was having a dinner party. It never arrived, however, so we were unable to see how much truth there might be in the rumours that the wind can cause a nervous disorder that resembles madness.

Strict controls on building development have helped preserve Pantelleria's Arabic appearance. Away from the island's harbour capital, the majority of the houses are still the traditional Arab *dammusi*, built with thick walls of black volcanic stone and whitewashed domed roofs.

The legacy of Pantelleria's violent volcanic past provides several natural attractions. From the 836m/2,743ft peak of Montagna Grande there are spectacular views over to Africa and all around the island. On the way down, near the village of Siba, we left the car and walked along the hillside. At an outcrop of rock there are caves filled with steam that has escaped from the volcano, creating a natural sauna. We stripped off and let the steam into our pores, a very relaxing and cleansing experience. As we stepped back into the daylight, the day that we had thought so warm seemed refreshingly cool. There is more volcanic activity along the coast. Hot springs bubble up in natural rock pools right next to the sea at Gadir and even underwater in the sea at Punto Nika.

**Anise**
**(*Pimipinella anisum*)**
The oval, aromatic seeds from anise, a herb closely related to cumin and fennel, were important to the very early trade from their native Levant. Phoenician sailors would have been the first to distribute them around the Mediterranean.

Anise has become part of daily life in Greece and Turkey as the main flavour in the national drinks of ouzo and arak. The flavour is also popular in stews, soups, breads, biscuits and sweets in Spain, Portugal, Germany and Italy. In Afghanistan and India the seeds are used as a breath freshener. In India anise has become a part of some spice mixtures. And few British children escape the dubious pleasure of aniseed balls.

On the seashore at Cala dei Cinque Denti, just below our *dammuso*, we copied other picnickers by pouring olive oil into the tiny bowl-shaped holes in the rock lined with dried sea salt, and dipping fresh bread in.

The local crops include olives, grown on dwarf trees; heavy rocks are placed on the young trunks to encourage growth near to the ground, where there is some protection from the salty winds. *Zibbibo* grapes grown in protected ridges are used to make a fruity white wine, *pantescho*, or dried to raisins to make the stronger golden *passito* wine.

But the island's most famous crop is capers. Sold salted, they are blended with fresh herbs and olive oil to make a delicious tapenade. They are also a vital ingredient in a wide variety of other local dishes.

*The **dammusi** of Pantelleria use a system of linked whitewashed roofs to collect rainwater for storage in underground tanks.*

## BAKED MONKFISH WITH CAPERS, FLAT-LEAF PARSLEY AND THYME

SERVES 4

115g/4oz dry salted capers
2 large garlic cloves, chopped
4 tablespoons olive oil
zest and juice of 1 lemon
2 tablespoons dry white wine

handful of flat-leaf parsley
8 sprigs of fresh thyme
4 200g/7oz monkfish fillets
4 knobs of butter

Pre-heat the oven to 200°C/400°F/gas 6. Rinse the capers under a tap and dry with kitchen paper. Combine them with the garlic, olive oil, the lemon zest and juice, white wine, parsley and thyme. Place the monkfish fillets on a baking tray and pour the sauce over them. Put a knob of butter on each fish and bake for 20 minutes.

## CAPER AND BLACK OLIVE SPICED TAPENADE

SERVES 4

175g/6oz dry salted capers
175g/6oz pitted black olives
2 garlic cloves, chopped
1 teaspoon dried oregano

6 tablespoons olive oil
1 red chilli, chopped
ground black pepper

Rinse the capers under a tap and dry with kitchen paper. Blend all the ingredients in a food processor until finely chopped, taking care not to make the mixture too smooth. Store the tapenade in a refrigerator.

## RED PEPPERS STUFFED WITH SPICED TAPENADE

SERVES 4

4 red peppers, cut in half and seeded
4 garlic cloves, chopped

caper tapenade (see above)
olive oil

Pre-heat the oven to 200°C/400°F/gas 6. Lay the peppers on a baking tray. Place some of the garlic and the tapenade inside each and bake for 1 hour. This dish goes perfectly with the baked monkfish recipe above.

**Capers
(*Capparis spinosa*)**
Capers are the green edible flower buds of a spiny trailing Mediterranean perennial shrub. The buds are always picked unripe and then pickled in vinegar. Unlike other spices of the region, such as fennel and cumin, capers cannot be dried, so they were not widely traded along early spice routes. However, they remain popular all around the Mediterranean, especially as accompaniments to fish and seafood dishes.

*Baked monkfish with capers, flat-leaf parsley and thyme, served with red peppers stuffed with spiced tapenade*

# campania

In a field of poppies at Paestum, on the Cilento coast of Campania in southern Italy, great sand-coloured pillars stand in perfect symmetry, supporting the remnants of a fifth-century Greek temple dedicated to Poseidon, god of the sea. Paestum was a busy centre of trade for Magna Graecia, the Greek settlement that included most of Italy south of Naples and all of Sicily. The use of fennel seeds from Greece and the eastern shores of the Mediterranean, and pepper from India's Malabar Coast, now so common in Italian cuisine, goes right back to this trading heyday. Although fennel has always grown abundantly in the region, the use of the seeds as a spice was a Greek introduction.

Just south of Paestum is the village of Castellabate, where, in the alfresco Belvedere restaurant of the Palazzo Belmonte, we ate this unusual combination of large salt-water prawns with white wine, brandy and fennel seeds.

## PRAWNS WITH FENNEL SEEDS AND BRANDY

SERVES 4–6

| | |
|---|---|
| 2 tablespoons butter | handful of flat-leaf parsley, chopped |
| 1 onion, finely chopped | salt and ground black pepper |
| 4 garlic cloves, finely chopped | 1 teaspoon fennel seeds |
| 500g/18oz king prawns | 200g/7oz tomato passata |
| 110ml/4fl oz white wine | 2 tablespoons crème fraîche |
| 2 tablespoons brandy | zest of a lemon |

Melt the butter in a large frying pan. Add the onion and garlic and fry until soft. Add the prawns and cook them on both sides for 2 minutes.

Add the white wine and brandy and cook with the parsley, and salt and pepper to taste, until the alcohol has evaporated. Next add the fennel seeds and the passata with 110ml/4fl oz of water and continue cooking for about 15 minutes.

Before serving, mix the crème fraîche and lemon zest diluted with a little water and pour over the prawns.

**Fennel
(Foeniculum vulgare)**
Native solely to the eastern Mediterranean, fennel has travelled extensively. Plants grown for seed were traded all over the Middle East into India and on to China and Southeast Asia.

In China fennel is one of the essential spices in the ubiquitous five-spice mixture, as it is in Bengal in *panch phoron*. In India fennel seeds are chewed, sometimes coated with sugar candy, as a breath freshener after a meal. They also feature in the paan masala mixtures wrapped in a betel leaf to accompany the mildly narcotic betel nut. Meanwhile, in fennel's region of origin, both the seeds and the vegetable root are still commonly used to flavour fish dishes, as they have been since ancient times.

*Prawns with fennel seeds
and brandy*

# the indian
# subcontinent

There were many overland spice routes in the north of the Indian subcontinent, but the south is more historically significant. The ports of the Malabar Coast (the region, roughly, from Goa south to Cape Comorin), especially those in Kerala in the far south, had the greatest influence on the trade routes of antiquity. From early times Egyptian, Roman and Chinese sailors engaged in maritime trade with southern India and Sri Lanka in search of pepper and cinnamon. The Arab discovery of useful and predictable seasonal monsoon winds in the first century AD reduced the sailing time between the eastern Mediterranean and the Malabar to a couple of months. Winds also took Malabar traders east into the Bay of Bengal, past the Irrawaddy delta and on to the Java Sea.

For centuries, Malabar Coast ports were of major importance to world trade, not only because they were close to the only source of pepper, but also because they were centres of transshipment and exchange for numerous spices and products between east and west. With this exchange of spice goods came cultural exchange too. The great civilizations of the Khmer in Cambodia (builders of Angkor Wat), the Shailendra Dynasty in Indonesia (builders of Borabudur), and the Majapahit empire of eastern Java all looked to southern India.

Jews, Christians (the origin of pre-Catholic Christianity in Kerala is attributed to the arrival of the apostle Thomas soon after the Crucifixion), Arabs, Gujaratis, Jains, Persians and Chinese all settled in their own trading communities along the Malabar Coast, and spice routes were established inland as well as across oceans. The Hindu dynasties that ruled over affluent civilizations across southern India throughout the first millennium AD and beyond, all made widespread use of the spices of the Malabar Coast.

Sea links between the Malabar ports and China, which had existed from Roman times, were well established by the time of the thirteenth-century rule of Kublai Khan, whose envoy Marco Polo spent time there.

PAGES 48–49: *Melas, or fairs, have for centuries attracted tens of thousands of pilgrims. These Rajput pilgrims have gathered at the desert oasis of Pushkar in Rajasthan for an auspicious bathe under a full moon.*

LEFT: *The pilgrims at this* mela *are bathing in a tributary of the Ganges. This annual event at Sonepur in Bihar is also the site of India's largest elephant market, the Hathi Bazaar.*

ABOVE: *This mural on a wall in Shekhawati, Rajasthan, depicts the traditional caravans of camels along the desert spice routes of western India and the trains that eventually replaced them.*

RIGHT: *One of the oldest overland spice routes made its way through the Karacoram Mountains, crossing the Himalayan barrier, linking China and Central Asia with the lands of the Indus and the ports of the Arabian Sea. This photograph shows the Hunza Valley, close to the modern border between China and Pakistan.*

The arrival of European merchant ships, first from Portugal in the fifteenth century, then from Holland in the seventeenth century and Britain in the nineteenth, only served to strengthen and confirm the independence of Keralan spice suppliers. In the sixteenth century pepper still accounted for over 70 per cent by volume of the world spice trade.

The Taj Mahal, built in the seventeenth century, may be the most famous image of Mughal rule in India; for most people of India's northern states, however, the most tangible legacy of that time is Mughal cuisine and spice mixtures, many of which still feature in their diet and make up what we think of as typical Indian food. By the time of Akbar the Great (1542–1605), the Mughals' power stretched as far as the ports of Gujarat and Bengal, giving them direct access to the sea-borne spices from Malabar, and the new ones arriving with the Portuguese.

The Portuguese can claim to have been responsible for the single most important change in the spicing of Indian food, by introducing chillies from the Americas to the Malabar and Goa. Before long a passion for chillies had spread throughout India and the land became self-sufficient in chilli production.

Though Indian textiles became increasingly controlled by the English East India Company, the native traders of the Malabar and Sri Lanka made far more out of the spice trade than any European interlopers. Spices shipped up from the Malabar to the ports of Gujarat on the Arabian Sea and Bengal on the Ganges delta, were mixed with local spices of the Gangetic Plain and the Himalayan foothills and spices arriving from the west with the Muslim invaders to produce some of the masala mixtures familiar in Indian cooking today.

As the Mughal empire retreated it was replaced by British administration of large parts of India. The south held out longest against manipulation or interference by the foreigners, but by 1857 Britain had declared India part of its empire. The most significant effect of this period on the spice trade was the establishment by the British of communities of Indians as indentured labourers, merchants and administrators in all their other colonies. Millions from the Punjab, Gujarat, Bengal, Tamil Nadu and other areas left India never to return. The well-established Indian communities that now live all over the world have brought their traditions of highly spiced cooking with them.

the malabar coast

The idea of leaving a 'margin of error' takes on a whole new meaning on Indian roads. Indian drivers like to operate within a hair's-breadth margin of error that does not always make the difference between uninterrupted progress on a relatively normal journey, and a 'traffic incident'. Traffic incidents at their best are likely to mean time-wasting, frustrating delays, and involve a lot of shouting. At their worst, as all too often reported in the Indian press, they mean carnage. For the insurers of international car hire firms, this margin of error is not good enough: despite a huge tourist industry India has almost no facilities for self-drive car hire. Our drive around Kerala, as passengers in a fine old Hindustani Ambassador, was chauffeured by an amiable Cochin Christian called Christopher. It felt like a pilgrimage: a visit to the single richest source of spices in the history of the trade, the Cardamom Hills of Malabar.

We had already seen the country we were to drive through, from the air. The Western Ghats rise above the steamy Malabar Coast of southern India to cooler heights, where tea, coffee and spice plantations form

LEFT: *The Chinese style of these fishing nets, still used at Cochin, dates back to the time of Kublai Khan in the thirteenth century, when Chinese merchants settled on the Malabar Coast to engage in spice trading.*

ABOVE: *Although buildings like this one are evidence of Cochin's historic spice trade, most of the modern trade takes place on a massive commercial scale in the container docks at Ernakulam nearby.*

patchwork patterns between tracts of forest. The spices that made Cochin such a prosperous port, linking it with China, Java, Arabia and Europe over three millennia, came from these tropical forests. They are the home of the pepper vine, which climbs betel, palm and mango trees to produce bunches of little berries. When picked unripe and dried in the sun, these become black peppercorns, the most valuable and internationally traded spice of the early trade routes.

We stopped for lunch in Kottayam, a provincial town at the beginning of the winding route into the hills, and found it thick with churches. These all have large hoardings outside proclaiming the exact type of Christianity they represent. The variety is astonishing. There are Jacobite churches, Mar Thoma churches, some are Syrian Orthodox, others Orthodox Syrian, there is a Protestant Church of South India and a Syrian Catholic Church, there is St Mary's Big Church just down the road from St Mary's Small Church (which is by far the bigger of the two).

Leaving this kaleidoscope of Christians, we made our way up into the Cardamoms, past hillsides of tea bushes busy with swarms of slow-moving pickers, and crossing rivers alive with the rhythm of washing being beaten into submission, the rocky banks covered by a vivid patchwork of drying saris. By the time we were in spice country, it was getting dark and we were glad that it was Christopher negotiating the bends.

The next morning our enthusiasm for buying spices in the bazaar of the small town of Thekkady led to an invitation to visit the spice garden of a local family. Here the native cardamom, turmeric and pepper grew prolifically alongside imported ginger, cloves, nutmeg, cinnamon, chillies, cumin and coriander. The family operates a cottage industry, preparing the spices for sale in a small shop down in the bazaar. They are in a competitive trade. The conditions for growing spices are so favourable up here that every home has its spice garden, and the shops of Thekkady are piled high with bags of freshly ground spices, each blend claiming to be a unique and secret recipe handed down by generations of family cooks. After our garden tour our hospitable new friends invited us to dinner. We enjoyed, and learned to cook, *koghi nadan* curry, a Keralan dish of chicken with fresh mangoes and curry leaves in a coconut milk sauce.

*The backwater canals of Kerala can be difficult to navigate when they become choked with water hyacinth. Small boys, however, are little hindered in their need to get to the other side.*

# KERALAN HOME-STYLE CHICKEN WITH COCONUT, MANGO AND CURRY LEAVES

SERVES 4–6

1 dessertspoon coriander seeds
1/2 teaspoon black peppercorns
1/2 teaspoon turmeric
5 tablespoons sunflower oil
1 dessertspoon black mustard seeds
1 large red onion, chopped
3 garlic cloves, finely chopped
2.5cm/1in cube of fresh ginger, peeled and finely chopped

12 curry leaves
800g/1lb 12oz chicken breast, cut into strips
1 dessertspoon white wine vinegar
400ml/14fl oz coconut milk
2 large mangoes, peeled, stoned and cubed
salt to taste

In a small pan dry-roast the coriander seeds and black peppercorns until they become aromatic. Remove them from the heat and grind to a powder. Combine them with the turmeric and set to one side.

In a large wok, heat the oil and fry the mustard seeds until they crackle. Add the onion, garlic, ginger and curry leaves, and fry until the onions become translucent. Add the chicken and fry until golden brown.

Add the coriander, black pepper and turmeric spice mix, and fry for 1 minute, stirring constantly to avoid sticking. Add the vinegar and 125ml/4fl oz of water and simmer for 2 minutes. Add the coconut milk and the mango cubes and salt to taste. Gently simmer for a further 5 minutes, taking care not to allow the coconut milk to boil.

Serve with rice and pea and potato masala (see page 61).

We came across more recipes when we swapped our car for a boat to explore the labyrinth of canals, lagoons, rivers and lakes that make up the backwaters of Kerala behind the Malabar Coast. Comfortably accommodated on a converted rice barge, we were fed on crispy masala fish, creamy coconut curries, spicy vegetable thorans, succulent tropical fruits and cold beers as we drifted quietly through the lives of farmers, fishermen and ferrymen. Everything was absurdly picturesque, seemingly unhurried and happy. At night we moored in the middle of a quiet lake, for more breeze and fewer mosquitoes, our lives feeling pretty unhurried and picturesque too by now. A dish of king prawns cooked with Keralan spices and fresh coconut was our moonlit supper.

**Pepper
(*Piper nigrum*)**
For centuries, pepper was the most important spice traded internationally. *Piper nigrum* is native to the Malabar Coast of India. Although it now grows in much of Southeast Asia, tropical Africa and Brazil, the ports of the Malabar grew rich from a long monopoly in supply. The value of pepper was so high by the end of the Roman Empire that in 410, Alaric the Goth demanded 3,000lb of it as part of his price to spare Rome.

The spice grows on a perennial vine. The berries are picked unripe. Some are pickled and sold as green pepper, but most are dried in the sun and graded by sifting or sorting to produced the familiar black peppercorns. When these are crushed and eaten they increase the flow of saliva and gastric juices, stimulating appetite and enlivening taste buds.

Alternatively, the berries are sometimes allowed to ripen. They are then soaked to remove the outer husk and dried to make the hotter white pepper.

There are other types of pepper. Long pepper, (*Piper sylvaticum*), also from India, grows like catkins, is hotter but not an easy spice to export as it is moister and prone to mould. By the sixteenth century this type of pepper had been ousted by the much more versatile chilli.

Sichuan pepper from China, melegueta pepper from Africa, Jamaican pepper (allspice) from the Caribbean, and all the chilli peppers from Mexico and Peru are completely unrelated to *Piper nigrum*.

*Keralan home-style chicken with coconut, mango and curry leaves*

# MALABAR PRAWNS

*This recipe uses fresh coconut. If you have never prepared a coconut before this is how to do it. At the bottom of the coconut are three 'eyes': with a corkscrew or skewer make a hole through one of the eyes, pour out and retain the coconut water, place the coconut in a plastic bag, put it on the floor and hit it with a hammer or a rolling pin. Remove the coconut flesh from the shattered shell.*

SERVES 4

| | |
|---|---|
| 1 tablespoon coriander seeds | 1 teaspoon black mustard seeds |
| 1 teaspoon fennel seeds | 10 curry leaves |
| 4 tablespoons sunflower oil | 1½ teaspoons tamarind purée, |
| 1 medium red onion, chopped | dissolved in 225ml/8fl oz of boiling |
| 2.5cm/1in cube of fresh ginger, peeled | water |
| and roughly chopped | 8oz/225g marrow, peeled, deseeded |
| 4 red chillies, deseeded and roughly | and cubed |
| chopped | 2.5cm/1in cube of jaggery or |
| ½ a fresh coconut, finely sliced | 1 dessertspoon brown sugar |
| (see above) | salt to taste |
| water from the coconut | 350g/12oz fresh prawns |

In a small pan, dry-roast the coriander and fennel seeds. When they become aromatic, remove from the heat and grind to a powder.

In a large wok, heat the oil and add the onion, ginger, chilli and sliced coconut. Fry gently until the ingredients become golden brown.

Remove from the pan with a slotted spoon and place in a blender with the ground coriander and fennel and the retained coconut water. Blend until a paste forms.

Fry the mustard seeds and curry leaves in the oil that remains in the wok. When the seeds crackle, add the coconut paste and fry for 1 minute, stirring constantly. Add the tamarind water along with the marrow and jaggery and salt to taste, bring to the boil then reduce the heat and simmer gently for 5 minutes. Add the prawns and continue to simmer until they are cooked.

Serve with rice.

## Jaggery
### (*Caryota urens*)

Jaggery is a palm sugar collected as sap from palm trees and used as a sweetener, often in combination with either amchoor or tamarind, to produce a sweet and sour flavour to dishes. Despite a very low sugar content jaggery is very sweet and has a fudge-like quality, making it an interesting alternative to sugar. It is not really a spice and is of little importance to the spice routes. It does, however, give a characteristic taste to cooking of the subcontinent and Southeast Asia, and today is exported all over the world to shops specializing in Asian cookery. It is sold as bricks wrapped in plastic or in jars.

## Tamarind
### (*Tamarindus indica*)

The pod clusters of the tamarind tree contain seeds and a dark brown sticky pulp. This is used as a souring or acidifying agent in cooking, often blended with sugar or jaggery (palm sap), to produce a sweet and sour effect. Although associated mostly with India where it is widely grown and its use is prolific, the tamarind tree was originally native to eastern Africa. Despite having become a popular ingredient all over Asia, the Caribbean and much of Latin America, its use is limited in eastern Africa. By the time the spice trade was developing the tree was already well established in India, so it was never a lucrative export for Africa.

**Cardamom
(Elettaria cardamomum)**
Cardamom's home is the tropical forests of the hilly Western Ghats that rise above the Malabar Coast of India, romantically known as the Cardamom Hills. The small green pods contain three chambers of tiny black seeds and grow along the ground under thick bushes. Its cultivation is inevitably costly making it the third most valuable spice, after saffron and vanilla.

Its use in India is widespread in creamy sweets like *ras malai*, in ice creams like *kulfi*, in spiced tea (*chai masala*), and as a breath freshener. In the biryani rice dishes of Hydrabad and of the once Mughal north, and in garam masalas, it is often used alongside the coarser, larger and more bitter black cardamom pods. The Arab traders who first transported cardamom to the west have developed a passion for it in coffee. It is either ground into roasted coffee beans or, in the case of the nomadic Bedu, inserted as a fresh pod into the spout of a coffeepot. Cardamom is now also grown in Sri Lanka, Tanzania and Guatemala.

## KERALAN GARAM MASALA

*One day we visited an Ayurvedic massage centre in the grounds of an antique colonial villa, in Kumarakom. Laiju Jameson, the chef at the restaurant there, taught us to make a delicious pea and potato side dish (see below). The recipe uses a Keralan garam masala made in the following way:*

3 green cardamom pods, shelled
3 cloves
2 bay leaves
1 teaspoon cumin seeds

2.5cm/1in piece of cinnamon stick
5 black peppercorns
½ teaspoon freshly grated nutmeg

In a small frying pan, dry-roast all the ingredients except the nutmeg until they are aromatic. Remove the spice mixture from the heat and grind to a powder. Combine with the grated nutmeg.

## KERALAN PEA AND POTATO MASALA

SERVES 4

500g/1lb 2oz waxy potatoes, peeled and cubed
60g/2oz cashew nuts
1 dessertspoon coriander seeds
1 teaspoon chilli powder
½ teaspoon ground turmeric
4 tablespoons sunflower oil
1 large onion, chopped
4 garlic cloves, chopped

2.5cm/1in cube of fresh ginger, peeled and grated
200g/7oz tomatoes, pulped in a food processor
225g/8oz shelled fresh peas
Keralan garam masala (see above)
1 tablespoon thick cream
salt to taste
handful of coriander leaves, chopped

Boil the potatoes until soft, drain, and set aside. Combine the cashew nuts with 2 tablespoons of water in a blender to make a paste, then stir in 150ml/5fl oz of water.

In a small frying pan, dry-roast the coriander seeds until they become aromatic, then remove them from the heat and grind to a powder. Combine with the chilli powder and the ground turmeric.

In a large pan, heat the oil and add the onion, garlic and ginger. Fry until the ingredients are golden brown. Add the coriander, turmeric and chilli mixture and fry for 30 seconds, stirring constantly to prevent sticking.

Add the pulped tomatoes, bring to the boil, then gently simmer until the oil returns. Add the cashew nut paste followed by the cooked potatoes and the peas and gently simmer until the peas are soft.

Stir in the garam masala, cream and salt to taste, and garnish with the coriander leaves.

# bombay

Bombay – now officially known by its Hindi name, Mumbai – did not exist as a city when the Portuguese first arrived on the west coast of India in search of spices. Where India's richest city and busiest port now stands as a centre of world trade, there was just a group of seven marshy, malarial islands occupied by Koli fishermen. Only one of these islands, now known as Elephanta, had an earlier history as the short-lived capital of a seventh-century Hindu dynasty which constructed beautiful cave temples. Remains of the magnificent carvings and paintings can be seen to this day.

When the British became the dominant foreign power in India, seeing off the Portuguese and Dutch, and established influence by conquest and compromise over local rulers, they revitalized old trade routes to the Deccan – the land south of the Narmada river – and beyond. The land around the islands was drained and reclaimed, Parsi and Gujarati merchants moved in, and a thriving port developed. When the Suez Canal opened in 1869, Bombay eclipsed Calcutta as India's primary port.

We are lucky enough to have several friends in Bombay, among them Gujarati Jains, Zoroastrian Parsis, Muslim Bengalis, Punjabi Sikhs, Catholic Goans and Hindu Maharashtrians. In their homes and favourite restaurants we have been treated to some of the best and most diverse food anywhere in India. The melting-pot nature of Bombay has to some extent eroded caste and religious bigotry among the city's population. Some people, however, are still strict about certain forbidden foods or have intransigent tastes concerning the degree and style of spicing, while others just prefer home cooking. To cope with all this, an ambitious and extraordinarily successful system for delivering freshly cooked food from suburban kitchens to office desks is organized by the Guild of Bombay Tiffinbox Suppliers' Association. Armies of quick-witted, athletic *dabba-wallas* manage to negotiate the seething streets and railway carriages of Bombay with thousands of three-tiered aluminium lunchboxes and deliver the right *dabba* to the right office worker every working day.

*Old and new types of transport in the busy streets of Bombay, where the traffic is often so congested that elephants are the quickest method of getting around.*

## BOMBAY DHANSAK MASALA

*This is the correct amount of masala mix for the dhansak chicken recipe that follows. Dhansak is a spice mixture typical of Parsi cooking: a garam masala that features fenugreek leaves and star anise.*

1 dessertspoon coriander seeds
1 teaspoon cumin seeds
5 black peppercorns
4 green cardamom pods, shelled
4 cloves
3 star anise seeds

2.5cm/1in piece of cinnamon stick
2 bay leaves
1 teaspoon black mustard seeds
1 teaspoon chilli powder
1 dessertspoon dried fenugreek
   leaves

In a small frying pan, dry-roast all the ingredients except the chilli powder and the fenugreek leaves until they become aromatic. Remove from the heat and grind to a powder. Combine with the chilli and fenugreek leaves.

## PARSI DHANSAK CHICKEN

*This dish uses a combination of three types of dhal. If you can't find all three, simply use 230g/8oz of the ones you can find.*

Serves 4–6

230g/8oz of dhal made up of:
   110g/4oz toor dhal, or yellow split
      peas
   60g/2oz red split lentils
   60g/2oz mung dhal
1 teaspoon turmeric
5cm/2in piece of fresh ginger, peeled
   and grated
handful of fresh dill
225g/8oz butternut squash, peeled
   and diced
225g/8oz aubergine, cubed
4 tablespoons ghee or butter
1 large red onion, chopped

4 garlic cloves, finely chopped
2 green chillies, finely chopped
560g/1lb 4oz chicken breast, cut
   into strips
dhansak masala (see above)
3 large tomatoes, pulped in a blender
1 dessertspoon tamarind purée,
   dissolved in 225ml/8 fl oz boiling
   water
5cm/2in square of jaggery or
   1 tablespoon brown sugar
handful of coriander leaves, chopped
juice of a lime
salt to taste

In a saucepan combine the three dhals with the turmeric, ginger, fresh dill, squash, aubergine and 750ml/1½pts of water. Bring to the boil, cover the saucepan, reduce the heat and gently simmer until the vegetables are soft and the lentils begin to break down.

**Turmeric**
**(*Curcuma domestica*)**
The root (rhizome) of the turmeric plant is a native of Asia, where it is used as a cosmetic, a dye and a tool of religion as well as a spice. In India its use is prevalent in vegetarian food where its bright yellow colour makes dishes look more attractive. The taste is slightly peppery. Turmeric's yellow appearance has led to its being passed off in some places as the much more valuable and subtle saffron, (although some of this deception may be unintentional as the French for turmeric is *safran des Indes*). Turmeric has become a popular spice in North Africa and the Caribbean. It is also now grown in China, Indonesia, Peru and Australia.

**Ginger**
**(*Zingiber officinale*)**
Ginger has long been unknown in the wild, so it may have originated anywhere in Asia. However, its early place in the spice trade is as an export from the Malabar Coast to Arabia, Europe and China.
   In India the fresh root, or rhizome, is commonly used crushed or chopped with garlic as a fried base for wet dishes. In China it is more likely to be used as thin strips in stir-frys. It also has a long history of use as a cold cure, in a drink with honey and lemon. In Kashmir, ginger tea is a daily pleasure. The Portuguese brought ginger to West Africa where it is used to flavour groundnut stews and make ginger beer. The Spanish introduced it to Mexico and the Caribbean where people already passionate about the heat of chillies in food took readily to the addition of ginger. In North Africa and the Indian Ocean ginger is used in cooking as a powdered dry spice. In Europe, ginger has become well established as an ingredient of cakes, biscuits and bread.

Meanwhile, heat the ghee in a large wok. Add the onion, garlic and chillies, and fry gently until the onions caramelize. Add the chicken pieces and fry until golden brown, stirring regularly. Stir in the dhansak masala and fry for 1 minute. Add the pulped tomato, tamarind water, jaggery and coriander leaves, along with the cooked dhal and vegetables. Bring to the boil, reduce the heat and gently simmer for 10 minutes. Add the lime juice, and salt to taste. Serve with rice.

## BOMBAY FISH

*This dish combines fish with cashew nuts and spices in a buttery coconut sauce thickened with poppy seeds.*

### Serves 4

5 green cardamom pods, shelled
1 teaspoon fennel seeds
1 dessertspoon coriander seeds
1 teaspoon cumin seeds
2 strands of mace
1 teaspoon white poppy seeds
2oz/60g cashew nuts
1½oz/45g desiccated coconut
1 red onion, roughly chopped
3 garlic cloves, roughly chopped

3 fresh green chillies, seeded
large handful of chopped coriander
  leaves
5 stems of fresh mint
juice of 2 limes
2 tablespoons ghee or butter
6oz/175g podded fresh peas
salt to taste
4 7oz/200g fillets of chunky white fish

In a small frying pan, dry-roast the cardamom, fennel, coriander, cumin and mace until they are aromatic. Remove the spice mix from the pan, add the poppy seeds and grind it all to a powder. In the same pan, dry-roast the cashew nuts, and when they start to turn golden brown add the desiccated coconut. Continue roasting gently until the coconut is golden. Remove from the pan and put in a blender along with the spice mix, plus the red onion, garlic, chillies, coriander, mint, lime juice and 4 tablespoons of water. Blend to form a paste.

In a wok, heat the ghee and fry the paste for 1 minute, stirring constantly. Stir in 225ml/8fl oz of water to form a sauce, and add the peas and salt to taste. Gently lay the fillets across the bottom of the pan. Spoon the sauce over them and simmer until the fish is cooked through (about 8 minutes).

Serve immediately.

**The huge popularity of Bollywood film stars has inspired one Bombay photographer to set up life-sized figures of them on the beach and to charge fans to have their picture taken next to their screen heroes and heroines.**

# rajasthan and gujarat

The desert cities of Rajasthan became wealthy from the camel caravan routes linking India's Arabian Sea ports with Arabia, Persia and central Asia. Spices travelled in both directions. Gujarat's dhow harbours of Mandvi, Porbander and Veraval were busy in the fifteenth century unloading pepper, turmeric, cinnamon and cardamom from the Malabar Coast and reloading cumin, coriander and fennel from the eastern Mediterranean. One caravan route ran north to Bhuj, across the mudflats of the Rann of Kutch to Jaisalmer, then north to the Khyber Pass or west through the Thar Desert and Sind, over the Indus. Another ran northeast through Udaipur and Jodhpur, and through the Aravalli Hills, taking

spices to the Mughal capitals of Agra and Delhi, and later to Jai Singh's walled city, Jaipur.

My chance to find out more about the exciting tastes of Rajasthan came when I was commissioned to photograph the recently completed Raj Villas Hotel, a modern five-star hotel built in the style of an old Rajput palace. I stayed on long enough after I had completed my brief to attend the excellent cooking demonstration at the hotel, where I learnt how to make some of the dishes I had been enjoying elsewhere in Rajasthan. I also managed to squeeze in a magnificent head massage at the spa. This transported me to such a state of euphoria that I imagined my masseur to be skilled in some ancient eastern mystery of traditional healing. When it was over and I complimented him on his art, he cheerfully informed me that he was a graduate of a massage school in Tunbridge Wells in the south of England.

The spectacular twelfth-century fort of Jaisalmer, perched like a sand-castle on a hill overlooking the vast Thar Desert, was home to Rajput warriors and Jain merchants. The golden yellow citadel is still a living fortress of paved, winding, narrow alleys between palaces, temples and *havelis*. A contemporary trade in tourism has halted the city's long decline, but sadly this has brought new threats with it. The resident population has grown alongside tourism, putting unbearable pressure on the ancient infrastructures of water supply and drainage. Water seepage has penetrated and saturated the sandy foundations of the fort, and the castle has begun to collapse. Homes and palaces are in ruins and some people have been killed. In response to this tragedy, the Indian National Trust for Art and Cultural Heritage (INTACH), Jaisalmer in Jeopardy (a British registered charity) and World Monuments Fund USA have been active in raising funds and instigating programmes to alleviate the problems. In the winter of 1999 I travelled to Jaisalmer to attend and document a fund-raising weekend of festivities associated with this project.

My first visit to the castle had been twenty years earlier, arriving out of the desert after a seven-day camel trek across the Thar Desert from Bikaner. My friend Daniel and I spent these days becoming increasingly saddle-sore and unwashed in the company of our bad-tempered camels, inappropriately named Ladoo and Jelabi, after delicious Indian sweets, and two very good-humoured guides whose genial personalities probably owed a lot to their constant consumption of opium. We foolishly chose to undertake this journey in May, just as the pre-monsoon heat was reaching its zenith and the oases were running dry.

The nights cooking and sleeping under the stars were pleasant enough at first. Our guides cooked fine suppers and sang Rajasthani folk songs to us, often in the company of other desert-crossers sharing our camp. The best we could contribute was an out-of-tune version of 'I've been through the desert on a horse with no name'. To discourage snakes from sharing our bed we were advised to spread crushed onions over our skin every night. As there was never enough water to wash with, the morning sun baked the stale onion juice dry within minutes of rising, and our ability to remain fresh-faced deteriorated rapidly. The days became torture. Increasingly desperate for our adventure to end, we were torn between wanting to ride as much as possible every day and not wanting to ride at all because the camels were so uncomfortable and the sun so hot. Eventually we fell into our guides' habit of numbing ourselves to the hardships with a haze of opium-induced euphoria. By the time we caught

**ABOVE:** *A water seller waiting for business at a stopping point on a desert pathway.*

**PAGES 66–7:** *The sixteenth-century complex of Jain temples at Palitana overlooking the Gulf of Cambay and the desert beyond.*

**OPPOSITE:** *A woman passes designs painted on a wall inside the fort of Jaisalmer.*

our first glimpse of the longed-for Jaisalmer rising majestically out of the desert haze, the romance of the moment was compromised somewhat by our fuddled brains and dilapidated bodies.

My return could not have been more of a contrast, arriving on a specially chartered plane from Delhi, packed with affluent glitterati all donating fistfuls of rupees to support the Jaisalmer Conservation Initiative. A long weekend of events and entertainments had been organized to reward the donors. By day there were talks and tours, revealing the splendours of the city within the fort and numerous pavilions, temples, *havelis* and cenotaphs in the desert around it. At night there were sumptuous feasts, including one hosted by the Maharaja and Maharani of Jaisalmer at their remote water palace of Moolraj Sagar. By the light of a full moon (the timing was brilliant), we were treated to a pre-dinner evening raga sung by Shubha Mudgal, in a courtyard of gentle fountains and pools filled with thousands of rose petals, surrounded by hundreds of tiny ghee-burning lanterns.

## RAJASTHANI PUMPKIN DHAL

SERVES 4

300g/10oz masoor dhal, washed and
 soaked in water for 1 hour
pinch of salt
1/2 teaspoon sugar
1 teaspoon turmeric
1cm/1/2in square of fresh ginger,
 chopped
1/2 teaspoon ground cumin

300g/10oz pumpkin, chopped into
 1cm/1/2in cubes
juice of a lime
2 tablespoons ghee
1 teaspoon black mustard seeds
pinch of hing
2 garlic cloves, chopped
6 small dried red chillies

Bring 1.7l/3pts of water to the boil, add the soaked dhal, salt, sugar, turmeric, ginger, cumin and pumpkin and boil for 30 minutes. Remove from the heat, add the lime juice and blend in a food processor until smooth.

In a small pan melt the ghee and fry the mustard seeds, hing, garlic and chillies until the seeds have popped.

Stir the spice mixture into the dhal and serve.

*An elegant elephant carved in sandstone at the entrance to one of the Jain temples at Palitana in Gujarat.*

After our weekend of partying at Jaisalmer, we accompanied some Jain friends on the flight to Bhavnagar in Gujarat. About an hour by plane from the cosmopolitan bustle of Bombay, this is one of the most sleepy, undeveloped parts of India. Our friends were on a pilgrimage to climb the twin peaks of Mount Shatrunjaya, and perform *puja* (worship) at the beautifully carved white marble temples of Palitana at the summit.

Jains believe in the sanctity of all sentient beings. This necessitates a diet demanding not just strict vegetarianism, but also abstinence from all things that grow beneath the ground, for fear that harvesting them may harm creatures of the earth. White-clad Jain priests and nuns sweep the ground beneath their feet as they walk, and wear face-masks to ensure they cause no accidental harm to insects. Every Jain hopes once in their life to make the climb to visit Palitana and descend Mount Shatrunjaya.

*Camels like this bejewelled creature at the Pushkar oasis in Rajasthan are still used for desert transportation, but on nothing like the scale of the heyday of the trade caravans.*

**Hing
(Ferula assafoetida)**
The use of hing spread from Iran and Afghanistan to Ancient Greece and Imperial Rome. Today, however, it is used almost exclusively in Indian cookery, where it is famed as an antidote for flatulence, and is particularly popular in dishes using pulses and cauliflower.

It is collected as a sap from the rhizomes of certain giant fennel plants. The pungent, sulphuric smell of hing makes it seem an unlikely flavour enhancer. When sold as a powder it is often mixed with gum arabic and turmeric and referred to as 'yellow powder'. The food enhancement qualities of hing are not dissimilar to those of onion and the spice is popular with Jains, for whom root crops are taboo.

The Jains are a tiny minority among India's population of a billion, but generations of success as traders and merchants, stretching back to the early seafaring days of the spice trade, have elevated many to positions of wealth and influence disproportionate to their number. In expectation of regular demand, *dolleywallas* wait at the foot of the mountain offering, for a fee, to carry any pilgrim disinclined to toil. They do this in groups of four, using bamboo poles with a hammock suspended between them.

We did it the hard way as usual, setting off half-asleep at 4.30am to try and beat the heat. We failed: by the time we reached the summit five hours later we were nearly defeated. It was still the tail end of the monsoon in Gujarat, which is a quiet season for pilgrims, on account of increased insect activity on the paths. This meant no food or drink stalls at the top. By the time we got down again anything would have tasted delicious. First we drank copious glasses of fresh lime sodas with kal nemak (black salt), which is an excellent rehydration aid and surprisingly palatable in small quantities. Then we joined the *dolleywallas*, tucking into a Gujarati favourite, pau bhaji. Pau bhaji is like an Indian version of bubble and squeak. On a big round disc of steel heated by a naked flame, a mixture of mashed potato and vegetables sizzles away in ghee and spices. Around the outside are bread rolls cut in half and toasting, absorbing the spicy butter. It makes a sensational lunch for hungry pilgrims, although sadly our Jain friends could not join in, as they cannot eat potatoes.

## PAU BHAJI SPICE MIX

*A garam masala with the addition of amchoor and caraway seeds. This recipe gives enough to make both the pau bhaji and the pau bhaji chutney on page 74.*

| | |
|---|---|
| 3 bay leaves | 1 teaspoon caraway seeds |
| 1 dessertspoon coriander seeds | 1 teaspoon ground chilli |
| 1 dessertspoon cumin seeds | 1/2 teaspoon ground ginger |
| 2.5cm/1in piece of cinnamon stick | 1 teaspoon amchoor |
| 1/2 teaspoon black peppercorns | 1/4 teaspoon hing |
| 2 star anise seeds | |

In a small pan dry-roast the bay leaves, coriander, cumin, cinnamon, peppercorns, star anise and caraway until aromatic. Remove from the heat and grind to a powder. Combine with the remaining spices.

*Ideally suited to harsh desert environments, camels have been known to survive for seventeen days without water.*

## PAU BHAJI

SERVES 4

450g/1lb new potatoes, peeled and
  cubed
1/2 a medium cauliflower, cut into small
  florets
3 medium carrots, diced
150g/5oz podded fresh peas
150g/5oz green beans, topped and
  tailed and cut into 1cm/1/2in lengths
5 tablespoons sunflower oil
2 medium red onions, chopped

4 garlic cloves, finely chopped
3 tablespoons pau bhaji spice mix
  (see page 73)
450g/1lb tomatoes, pulped in a
  food processor
150g/5oz fresh spinach leaves, roughly
  chopped
2 handfuls of coriander leaves,
  chopped
6 soft bread rolls

In a saucepan boil the potatoes until soft. Remove from the heat and drain, then mash them with 85ml/3fl oz of water. Boil the cauliflower, carrots, peas and beans until soft, drain and set to one side.

In a large wok, heat the oil and fry the onion and garlic until the onion softens. Add the pau bhaji spice mix and stir well for 1 minute. Add the pulped tomatoes and spinach, bring to the boil then reduce heat. Simmer gently until the sauce reduces and the oil returns. Add the mashed potatoes, drained vegetables and salt to taste. Stir well to combine all the ingredients and gently cook on a low heat for 5 minutes.

Garnish with fresh coriander leaves and serve with tomato chutney (see below) and the soft bread rolls halved, toasted and buttered.

## TOMATO CHUTNEY FOR PAU BHAJI

2 garlic cloves, roughly chopped
2 green chillies, roughly chopped
2 large tomatoes, roughly chopped
handful of coriander leaves

1 heaped teaspoon pau bhaji spice
  mix (see page 73)
1 dessertspoon brown sugar
salt to taste

Place all the ingredients in a blender and blend to a smooth purée.

*Pau bhaji*

## GUJARATI DHOKLA

*This is a recipe for an unusual snack which could be served with drinks or as a starter. It is easy to make and quite delicious; whenever we serve it, it becomes a conversation piece. It is made with chickpea (gram) flour which is easily available in Asian/Middle Eastern shops and many supermarkets. In India, dhokla is usually made by mixing the gram flour with curds and allowing the batter to ferment in the sun for nine hours. Luckily there is a quick and easy alternative method using bicarbonate of soda and lemon juice. Dhokla is cooked by steaming. If you don't have a big enough steamer, you can improvise using a wok with a lid.*

SERVES 4–6

125g/4oz gram flour, sieved

1 teaspoon sugar

1/2 teaspoon salt

juice of a lemon

1 heaped teaspoon bicarbonate of soda

2 tablespoons sunflower oil

3 green chillies, finely sliced

2 teaspoons black mustard seeds

1 dessertspoon curry leaves

1 tablespoon desiccated coconut

handful of coriander leaves

1 teaspoon desiccated coconut

Grease a 23cm/9in cake tin. In a bowl mix the gram flour, sugar, salt and lemon juice. Gradually add 175ml/6fl oz of water, stirring well to prevent lumps forming. Now prepare the steaming vessel: pour water into the bottom of the steamer or the wok, cover with a lid, bring to the boil, then reduce the heat to a simmer. Place a stand in the water in the middle of the steamer.

Sift the bicarbonate of soda into the batter, stir well and pour immediately into the greased cake tin. Carefully lower the cake tin on to the stand, cover with a lid and steam for 20 minutes. Remove the cake tin and allow to cool for 10 minutes, then cut the *dhokla* into 5 × 2.5cm/2 × 1in diamond shapes.

Now make the spice tempering. In a small pan, heat the sunflower oil. When the oil is hot, add the sliced green chillies, followed by the black mustard seeds and curry leaves. Fry for 1 minute, add the desiccated coconut and continue frying until the coconut begins to turn brown. Remove from heat and pour evenly over the surface of the cooked *dhokla*.

Garnish with the coriander leaves and desiccated coconut. Lift out of the tin to serve.

*Gujarati dhokla*

# bengal

Bengal was tragically torn in half by the partition of India in 1947. Bengalis on the two sides of the artificial border share a language and traditions of cooking.

The area that was to be known as Bengal was incorporated into the early Mauryan and Gupta Buddhist empires before reverting to a long period of Hindu kingdoms that ended with the rule of Delhi sultans at the end of the twelfth century. The Islamic influence from the west began the conversions that 800 years later were to tear the state apart. Long before this, in 1341, Bengal had broken away from Delhi to form a separate sultanate. When the English East India Company chose to locate their centre of Asian operations at the Bengali port of Calcutta in the 1690s, it became one of the great trading cities of the world.

The friendly, gregarious and inquisitive nature of many Bengalis, combined with their passion for lively discussion, makes cafés and restaurants of the region places where even strangers are unlikely to feel lonely. *Panch phoron,* a spice mixture that Bengalis created out of local mustard seeds mixed with imported fenugreek, cumin, nigella and fennel, fried in ghee and added to vegetable masals and dhals, is popular on both sides of the border. We have eaten versions of the dish of *panch phoron* spiced vegetables (opposite) in Calcutta and Dacca.

## BENGALI PANCH PHORON SPICE MIX

Panch phoron *is a spice mix that gives a distinctive taste to dishes on both sides of the border that divides West Bengal from Bangladesh. The quantities given here make enough for the vegetarian recipe that follows. As the spices are stored whole, much more can be made and kept for other recipes.*

$^1/_2$ teaspoon nigella seeds

$^1/_2$ teaspoon yellow mustard seeds

$^1/_2$ teaspoon cumin seeds

$^1/_2$ teaspoon fennel seeds

$^1/_2$ teaspoon fenugreek seeds

Combine and use whole.

## BENGALI PANCH PHORON SPICED VEGETABLES

SERVES 4–6

225g/8oz yellow split peas

1 teaspoon turmeric

200g/7oz pumpkin, peeled, seeded and cubed

175g/6oz green beans, topped and tailed and cut into 2in/5cm lengths

200g/7oz mooli radishes, cut into cubes (if unavailable use regular radishes)

150g/5oz okra, topped and tailed and cut in half

1 tablespoon ghee

panch phoron (see above)

3 bay leaves

2 green chillies, finely chopped

1 dessertspoon brown sugar

salt to taste

In a large saucepan, combine the yellow split peas, turmeric and 1.25l/2pts water and bring to the boil. Reduce the heat and simmer gently with a lid on until the lentils start to break down. Skim off and discard any scum appearing on the surface. Add the pumpkin, beans, radishes and okra and simmer until they become soft.

In a small pan heat the ghee and crackle the *panch phoron*. Add the bay leaves and the chillies and fry until the chillies are soft. Remove from the heat and add to the vegetables and split peas.

Add the brown sugar and salt to taste, stir well and serve with rice.

*The wet delta lands of Bengal have always relied on river transport to distribute produce. When there is no wind, the crew resort to poles and oars.*

# sri lanka

Sri Lanka's role in the history of spices has been influenced primarily by the bark of a bushy evergreen tree of the laurel family, known as cinnamon. The island of Sri Lanka (formerly Ceylon) was once the world's sole source of cinnamon, a spice which has been important since antiquity. There is evidence that Ceylon was a starting point for spice routes as early as 1500 BC. Phoenician traders certainly dealt in cinnamon hundreds of years before Christ, and the Greek historian Herodotus wrote about it in the fifth century BC, assuming it to be a spice from Arabia. The early Arab spice merchants kept the true source secret for centuries. Once the Venetian–Mameluke monopoly on the spice routes between the east and Europe was broken by the Portuguese in the fifteenth century, finding the source of cinnamon was high on the new explorers' agenda. The Portuguese found Ceylon, and, aided by local unrest, gradually took over the entire island to establish their own monopoly on the trade. By the mid-seventeenth century this monopoly had been snatched by the Dutch East India Company. After about 150 years of successful Dutch rule, the British in turn occupied the island. Ceylon did not finally regain independence until 1948. Today, it is still a major world producer of cinnamon.

Sri Lanka's pivotal position on the spice routes is emphasized by the popular spice mixture called *suwanda kudu*, which blends native cinnamon with cloves from Indonesia, cumin, nigella and coriander from the eastern Mediterranean, and cardamom and fenugreek from India.

The cuisine of Sri Lanka shares several dishes and spice combinations with southern India, and this is not surprising, given Sri Lanka's high population of Tamils originating from Tamil Nadu in southern India. But there are many distinctively Ceylonese traditions in island cookery, including hoppers (rice flour pancakes), mallums (vegetable curries with curry leaves) and lots of delicious spicy chutneys.

*The vast tea estates of Sri Lanka's hill country divide the landscape into a patchwork of neatly trimmed tea bushes, factories and access roads.*

## SRI LANKAN SPICE MIX

*This roasted curry powder is typical of Sri Lanka. Traditionally, it is not cooked but added at the end of a recipe to add flavour. This recipe gives the right quantity to use in the dish of Sri Lankan spicy prawns (see opposite).*

1 teaspoon white rice
1/2 teaspoon coriander seeds
1/4 teaspoon cumin seeds
1 clove
1 green cardamom pod, shelled

1/4 teaspoon black mustard seeds
2.5cm/1in piece of cinnamon stick
1 heaped dessertspoon grated or
   desiccated coconut
3 curry leaves

**Fifth-century frescoes of young
women with offerings for the Buddha,
on the wall of a cave at Sigiriya, in
central Sri Lanka.**

In a small pan dry-roast the rice until it starts to brown. Add all the remaining ingredients and roast until the spices become aromatic and the coconut is golden brown. Remove from the heat and grind to a powder.

**Cinnamon**
(*Cinnamomum verum*)

Cinnamon was one of the first spices traded on international spice routes. For centuries, it was supplied by Arab traders, who closely guarded the source by creating elaborate myths to confuse the market. Both Herodotus in the fifth century BC and Theophrastus in the fourth century BC relate tales of daring involving the nests of terrible monstrous birds and valleys full of deadly snakes as possible sources of the aromatic dried bark. Sri Lanka has always been and continues to be the home of the best cinnamon, which is more delicate, sweeter and milder than cinnamon from any of the other producers. These today include the Seychelles, Réunion and South America. Cinnamon is also superior to the similar bark of the Chinese and Indonesian cassia trees with which it is often confused.

The spice is harvested by stripping away the outer bark of the cinnamon tree and then peeling off the inner bark as it dries and curls. These curls are inserted into each other according to size then shipped and sold as bundles.

The spice was popular among the Mexicans, who were introduced to it by the Spanish, and who used it to flavour their chocolate drinks, and also in eighteenth-century French cookery. In Morocco, cinnamon is used in tajines and through Asia Minor and Central Asia in pilaf. In Europe, cinnamon makes an annual appearance in winter in warm mulled wine and cider drinks. It is also used in baking and in stewing fruits and to flavour rice puddings

# SRI LANKAN SPICY PRAWNS

*This dish combines prawns with dill seeds and spinach and the typical Sri Lankan tastes of coconut and curry leaves.*

## SERVES 4

$1/4$ teaspoon black peppercorns
1 dessertspoon coriander seeds
1 teaspoon cumin seeds
$1/2$ teaspoon chilli powder
$1/4$ teaspoon turmeric
350ml/12fl oz coconut milk
400g/14oz fresh prawns
2 medium red onions, cut into thin
  semicircles

2 fresh green chillies, finely chopped
175g/6oz fresh spinach leaves, finely
  chopped
1 dessertspoon white wine vinegar
1 dessertspoon coconut oil
$1/2$ teaspoon dill seeds
15 curry leaves
salt to taste
Sri Lankan spice mix (see opposite)

In a small frying pan, dry-roast the black peppercorns, coriander and cumin seeds until they become aromatic, remove from heat and grind to a powder. Combine them with the chilli powder and turmeric in a large bowl and add a little water to make a paste. Stir in the coconut milk and 100ml/4fl oz of water, add the prawns, half of the red onion, the green chillies, the spinach and the white wine vinegar. Set to one side.

In a large wok, heat the coconut oil and fry the dill seeds and the curry leaves for a few seconds. Add the remaining red onion and fry until the onion softens.

Pour in the prawns and the spiced coconut milk, and gently simmer until the prawns are cooked, taking care not to boil the sauce as the coconut milk will separate.

Add salt to taste, remove from heat and sprinkle the Sri Lankan spice mix over the surface. Serve immediately with rice.

## SRI LANKAN OKRA AND POTATO CURRY

*In Sri Lanka curries are often described as white, to indicate mild spicing and use of coconut milk; red, to indicate the use of powerful red chillies and tomato; or black, when roasted spices are used. This is a white vegetable curry, which would typically include the use of 'Maldive fish', pounded dried fish in powdered form. As this is hard to find, we use Thai fish sauce.*

SERVES 4

| | |
|---|---|
| 400g/14oz baby new potatoes, cut into cubes | 2 teaspoons dill seeds |
| 20 curry leaves | 3 green chillies, finely chopped |
| ½ teaspoon turmeric | 300g/10oz okra, cut into 2.5cm/1 in chunks |
| 2 large red onions, cut into thin semicircles | 400ml/15fl oz coconut milk |
| 3 teaspoons Thai fish sauce | 2 dessertspoons lime juice |
| 3 tablespoons coconut oil | salt to taste |

In a saucepan, boil the potatoes in 350ml/12fl oz of water until soft, along with half the curry leaves, the turmeric, half the sliced red onions and the fish sauce.

Meanwhile, in a wok, heat the oil and add the dill seeds. When they start to crackle add the rest of the curry leaves followed by the chilli and the remaining sliced onion. Fry until the onion starts to turn golden brown. Add the okra and fry gently until they start to soften.

Add the boiled potato mixture (including the liquid), the coconut milk, the lime juice and salt to taste, with 125ml/4fl oz of water. Gently simmer for 5 minutes, taking care not to boil as the coconut milk will separate.

Add salt to taste and serve with rice.

**Curry Leaves**
(*Chalcas koenigii*)

Curry leaves, or *kari patta*, grow feather-like along a stem. In southern India and Sri Lanka they are often dropped into hot oil, along with mustard seeds, and added at the last minute as a tempering to vegetable dishes, dhals and chutneys. Trade in them has been limited, however. They are a common constituent of curry powders in the recipes of Indian Ocean islands and the Caribbean. It was the name of this leaf that European languages adopted as a generic term to describe all spiced dishes.

*Sri Lankan okra and potato curry*

# nepal

As Buddha Air Flight 200 from Kathmandu reached its climax, I just happened to be the passenger taking a turn at spending a couple of minutes squeezed between the pilots to admire the view. 'Complete top of the world,' said one of them, pointing through the perfect clarity of a Himalayan morning. Right in front of us was the distinctive pyramidal peak of Everest, all around us a vast snowscape of other peaks, valleys, glaciers and ridges of unparalleled dramatic grandeur. This was a once-in-a-lifetime's experience.

On my last trip to Nepal over twenty years ago, these Everest flights weren't an option. I experienced Everest the hard way, trekking with all my possessions on my back, sleeping in primitive teahouses and living off dhal and rice: it took weeks. That trek had also been a lifetime experience, although it didn't get me nearly so close to the summit. Flight 200 was cheating really. In fact our whole trip to Nepal this time round was a bit like cheating compared to my first. But we weren't here for the physical challenge; we had come to find Nepalese cuisine beyond dhal bhaat, among the mustard fields of the foothills.

Nepal grows 80,000 tons of mustard seed a year, supplying much of the vast demand across the border in India. The mustard fields are all far south of the Kathmandu Valley between the plains of the Terai and the Himalayas. The first interesting recipe we came across was a Newari dish we ate in a restaurant while still in Kathmandu. Newari food is traditionally very complex, reflecting the regal past of the Newars. Historically it has been a long way removed from the simple diet of most Nepalese. The emergence of a more affluent middle class around the Kathmandu Valley has inspired the inclusion of some of the less eccentric examples of Newari cuisine on Kathmandu menus. This one, called *panch kol*, is a spicy curry using five vegetables. In its spiciness it is typically Newari, but less typical for being meatless: the Newars have a tradition of cooking every part of a buffalo, as well as pork and venison.

*The peak of Mount Everest, 8,848m/29,028ft above sea level. Despite the extreme terrain, an ancient trade route was forged not far from here, linking La-sa in Tibet with Kathmandu.*

## PANCH KOL

*Panch kol is a combination of five vegetables — cauliflower, carrots, spinach, peas and radish — with a rich garlic and spiced-tomato gravy tempered with mustard seeds and sprinkled with an aromatic garam masala.*

### SERVES 4

**For the garam masala**
4 green cardamom pods, shelled
1 strand of mace
2 star anise
2.5cm/1in piece of cinnamon stick
4 cloves

1 large onion, roughly chopped
5 garlic cloves, roughly chopped
5cm/2in piece fresh ginger, peeled and
  roughly chopped
2 green chillies, roughly chopped
350g/12oz cauliflower, cut into small
  florets
200g/7oz carrots, diced
2 tablespoons mustard oil or ghee

1 dessertspoon sesame seeds
3 dried red chillies, chopped
1/2 teaspoon turmeric
400g/14oz tomatoes, pulped in a
  food processor
200g/7oz mooli, cut into cubes
  (or radishes, if unavailable)
150g/5oz podded fresh peas
175g/6oz fresh spinach, roughly
  chopped
1 dessertspoon brown sugar
1 dessertspoon mustard oil or ghee
1 tablespoon black mustard seeds
salt to taste
handful of chives, chopped
handful of fresh coriander leaves

Prepare the garam masala by dry-roasting the ingredients in a small frying pan and grinding to a powder.

Pulp the onion, the garlic, the ginger and the green chillies to a purée in a food processor. Parboil the cauliflower and carrots and set aside. In a large wok heat the mustard oil and fry the sesame seeds, dried red chillies and turmeric until the sesame seeds crackle. Add the onion purée and fry for a further 5 minutes, stirring regularly. Add the pulped tomato, bring to the boil, reduce the heat and simmer gently until the oil returns and the sauce reduces.

Add the mooli, the peas, the spinach and the brown sugar and simmer gently for 10 minutes more; add the drained parboiled vegetables and simmer for another 5 minutes.

Meanwhile, heat the mustard oil in a small frying pan. Add the mustard seeds and fry them until they crackle, then pour them on to the curry.

Finally, add salt to taste, sprinkle with garam masala, stir well and serve garnished with the chopped chives and coriander.

**ABOVE:** *A village in the Gorkha region of Nepal, perched on a hilltop in the morning sun.*

**OPPOSITE:** *A Gorkha woman on the terraced hillsides of Nepal.*

On our journey south from Kathmandu we visited Bhagwati Mandir, a favourite destination of Nepalese Hindus seeking divine favour. This temple, in the hilltop village of Manakamana, is dedicated to the goddess Bhagwati, who rewards pilgrimage and animal sacrifice with the granting of wishes. Until very recently this pilgrimage meant a long, hard trek up steep paths, with all the family, luggage and sacrificial beast in tow. As in many pilgrimages around the world, the effort required to get to Bhagwati Mandir would appear to have been part of the bargain of gaining merit through toil. The Nepalese, however, still find the journey meritorious enough, in spite of the recent construction of a gleaming new Austrian-built cable car. The overnight hike has been replaced by an easy two-hour round trip from the main road in the valley. Not only do more Nepalese make the pilgrimage now, but the temple also attracts coach- and carloads of Hindus from India and even a few foreign tourists.

The operation looks just like a ski resort in the Alps until it becomes apparent that in between some of the glass bubble capsules of the cable car are special open ones for animals with one-way tickets. At the top there are more goats and chickens for sale for anyone who is still not equipped for the ritual. The Indian Hindus do not sacrifice animals, so there are also stalls selling kits of coconut, rice, flowers and sweets for their version of appeasing Bhagwati. The pilgrims queue in family groups around the temple waiting for their time to enter the inner sanctum.

Those with animals, which on festival days or for big favours can include buffalo, are sure they are giving their victims a privileged departure from this world. A better chance for next time. They fondly stroke and whisper to the animals right up to the time a *sharki* caste temple butcher dispatches them with a swift decapitating stroke of his *khukhiri* knife. They are all going to be eaten anyway, and there is a thriving sub-industry around the temple in keeping braziers burning and in preparing dispatched animals for a family feast. Apart from the animals, the main victims of this modern style of pilgrimage are the empty teashops, food stalls and hostels that ran along the old trails.

The next stage of our trip took us away from the cool air of the mountains down to the humid jungles of southwest Nepal. Here, the only places to stay are jungle lodges associated with wildlife conservation parks like Chitwan and Bardia. These parks are beautiful areas of natural habitat for some of the last tigers, wild elephants, rhinoceroses and bears in the subcontinent, as well as many other less spectacular species. Much of the surrounding farmland is carpeted in vivid yellow mustard flowers.

There is a significant conflict of interests between the parks and the farmers. Wild animals can be deadly and may easily be tempted to help themselves to neat rows of healthy crops or domesticated farm animals. Many villagers have suffered the consequences of this uneasy equation. Possibly because of this, the villagers of the Terai, mostly poor farmers, are not as openly hospitable as the inhabitants of Nepal's mountain villages. The only places we found to eat were the kitchens of the lodges.

*A ranger in the Chitwan National Park, crossing a river in the pre-dawn mists that rise out of the jungle as the temperature climbs.*

Sadly, most of these attempt to provide a range of international dishes that takes them down some disastrous paths; but when the cooks produce their own food it is invariably excellent.

From our vantage point, high up on an elephant in Chitwan, the mountains were still visible as a wall of snow beyond the forest. Elephant rides give the unusual experience of fording deep rivers without getting wet, and passing through dense jungle getting very close to wild animals such as tigers, sloth bears and rhinoceroses, without getting killed.

In the evening we were taken to see the elephants sleeping. There were twenty or so, all snoring, lying on their sides and looking like giant grey boulders. From time to time each of the elephants in turn would rise to its feet and, hardly bothering to wake, grab a mouthful of straw, then settle down again on its other side. These massive creatures have to turn

*In the the flatlands of Nepal's Terai, most of the forest has been cleared to make room for carpets of yellow mustard flowers.*

**Mustard Seeds
(Brassica nigra)**

There are three main varieties of mustard, two of them native to Europe and the other to Asia. While the European varieties are traditionally ground with water to make a paste, the Asian brown mustard seeds are usually dried and added whole to dishes. The seeds may be fried in oil at the beginning of cooking vegetable dishes, dry-roasted and added at the end to salads and chutneys, or fried separately and added at the end to give a nutty flavour to dhals.

Most of the trade in these brown mustard seeds is confined to distribution within the Indian subcontinent from the carpets of yellow-flowered fields in the foothills of the Nepalese Himalayas. Mustard seeds are a particular feature of the dishes of Gujarat and the south.

over at regular intervals throughout the night to save their organs from being crushed under their immense weight.

In Bardia we saw a tiger kill a small deer right in front of us; the tiger's roar was blood-curdling. We had imagined that our elephant would keep us safe from anything, so were somewhat alarmed when it turned and fled, apparently motivated by the same primaeval fear as the roar awoke in us.

## NEPALESE BREAKFAST POTATOES

*One morning at the Narayani Safari Lodge on the edge of Chitwan we were served this wonderful Nepalese dish of potatoes cooked in a sweet mildly spiced tomato sauce. It made a perfect accompaniment to the fried eggs and locally grown forest mushrooms on offer. Even guests suspicious of the idea of 'curry for breakfast' enjoyed it.*

SERVES 4

750g/1½lb new potatoes, cut into
  small cubes
½ teaspoon turmeric
3 teaspoons ghee or butter
2 dessertspoons black mustard seeds
3 garlic cloves, finely chopped
225g/8oz tomatoes, pulped in a
  food processor
5cm/2in cube of jaggery or
  1 tablespoon brown sugar

2 dessertspoons coriander seeds and
  2 dessertspoons cumin seeds, dry-
  roasted until aromatic and ground
  to a powder
1 dessertspoon ghee or butter
2 dessertspoons cumin seeds
salt and pepper to taste
handful of coriander leaves, chopped

In a large saucepan, boil the potatoes along with the turmeric until they are soft. Drain and set to one side.

In a large wok, heat the ghee and add the mustard seeds. When they start to crackle, add the garlic, and fry until it browns. Add the pulped tomatoes, the jaggery and 350ml/12fl oz of water, bring to the boil, then simmer gently until the oil returns and the sauce reduces. Add the ground coriander and cumin, plus the drained potatoes, stir well and simmer gently for 5 minutes.

Meanwhile, in a small frying pan, heat 1 dessertspoon of ghee and fry 2 dessertspoons of cumin seeds until they crackle. Remove them from the heat and pour on to the potatoes.

Finally, add salt and pepper to taste and garnish with the chopped coriander leaves. Serve for breakfast with fried eggs and mushrooms.

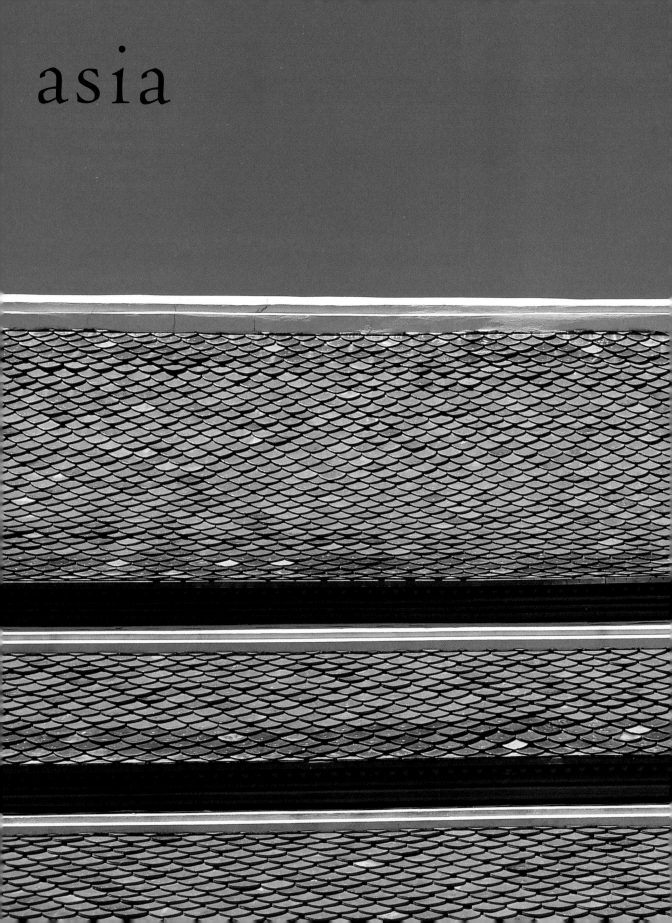

asia

The sea routes between the Malabar Coast of India, Arabia and the islands of the South China Sea were not the only early spice routes into and out of Asia. There were also long overland treks across the deserts and grasslands between China and the Arab lands of Asia Minor and the cities of the Mediterranean, as well as trails over the Himalayas and through the jungles between China and the Indian subcontinent.

China's main export was silk. The various trade routes to the west, either via Samarkand and the Tien Shan mountains or K'a-shih (Kashgar) and the T'a-k'ola-ma-khan Sha-mo (Takla Makan Desert), began at the time of Confucius (551–479 BC) and became known as the Silk Routes. These routes were in turn connected by the passes across the Karakoram and Pamir mountain ranges to the ports of the Indus and Ganges in India. As well as bringing pepper from India, China also had an extensive maritime trade with the Spice Islands of Southeast Asia, from which it brought cloves and nutmegs. From the west came previously unknown spices like fennel and sesame, both of which remain essential ingredients in Chinese cookery.

In 1271 Marco Polo began a twenty-four-year trip from Venice overland to China and Burma, then back by sea via Southeast Asia, the Malabar and Gujarat ports of India and the Persian Gulf. The trade links he established between the emerging Italian city state and the Far East helped Venice grow into the richest and most powerful city in Europe during the fourteenth and fifteenth centuries.

The Ming dynasty that replaced Mongol power in China maintained these links to Europe and the outside world, and by the fifteenth century their ships were reaching ever more distant shores. The greatest of the Chinese navagators was Cheng Ho (c. 1371–1435). Under the patronage of the Emperor Yung-lo he embarked on a series of expeditions that were to link China with ports as far away as Melaka, Zanzibar and even Mecca. He sailed in fleets of massive treasure junks, the largest and most sophisticated wooden sailing ships ever built.

PAGES 94–95: *Temple rooftops of intricate design and colour brighten the skyline of Bangkok, the only port city of Asia that resisted colonial occupation throughout the era when Europeans dominated the spice trade.*

RIGHT: *The country roads between the Huang Shan Mountains in China are popular with cyclists.*

Chinese merchants settled in foreign ports with trading rather than colonial ambitions, starting a tradition of China Towns around the world. Chinese spices became established in cuisines all around the Indian Ocean and South China Sea, and Chinese cooking became increasingly influenced by the reliable supply of spices from Europe, Arabia, India and Southeast Asia.

Halfway through the fifteenth century, expeditions were halted by the Chinese under a new policy of isolationism. Eventually all foreign travel was declared illegal and Cheng Ho's maps and journals were destroyed to discourage other merchant explorers. The timing of this was very significant. The European demand for spices was still increasing and the high prices enforced by the Venetian–Mameluke monopoly inspired the great age of maritime exploration by the Portuguese and Spanish. The end of Chinese naval power and exploration left the spice lands of Southeast Asia particularly vulnerable to European exploitation.

The Portuguese arrived first, capturing Melaka in 1511 on their way to Macao, which in 1557 became the first European conquest in China. The Spanish were close behind, arriving from the other direction via recently discovered America. They reached the all-important Spice Islands (as the Moluccas were then known) in 1527, but concentrated on colonizing the Philippines and converting their inhabitants to Catholicism. Portuguese domination of the Southeast Asian spice routes was relatively short-lived; the major impact they made on the region was the introduction of the American chilli, radically changing the spicing of local cuisine.

The Dutch had a much greater influence on the Spice Islands, although even they faced fierce competition from the English. Before the end of the sixteenth century, Holland's sea trade had consisted solely of collecting spices from Lisbon to distribute around the Baltic ports. But the anti-Catholic campaigns of William of Orange led to Dutch ships being banned from Portuguese and Spanish ports and waters, forcing the Dutch to find their own way to the source of spices. They achieved this in 1597, a fleet returning having lost more than two-thirds of its crews to scurvy and other hazards, but packed with valuable cloves, nutmegs and mace. The Portuguese monopoly was broken.

The Dutch soon organized themselves into efficient world traders. The merchants of Amsterdam banded together to form the Dutch East India Company and convoys of heavily armed flotillas set sail for the Spice Islands. Much of Philip of Spain's fleet had been destroyed by the English in 1588, and lone Portuguese ships made easy targets. Indian,

**ABOVE:** *The heavy rainfall and hot tropical sun of Indonesia provide the perfect conditions for the growth of spices as well as of rice and vegetable crops.*

**OPPOSITE:** *A typical scene of terraced rice paddy farming on the Indonesian archipelago.*

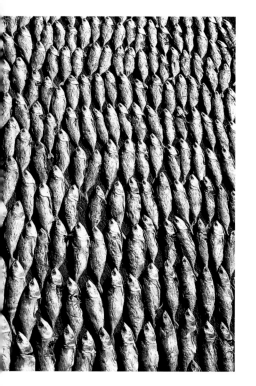

ABOVE: *Nowhere in Indonesia is far from the sea, so fish plays a big part in the cuisine of the islands. Markets typically have impressive displays, like this one on a stall in Lombok.*

OPPOSITE: *A waterfall in the lush jungle interior of the Indonesian island of Lombok.*

Malay, Javanese and Arab craft posed little challenge. Only the English gave the Dutch a run for their money. The first Englishman to reach the Spice Islands was Francis Drake in 1579, having sailed westwards, around South America through the Strait of Magellan, and across the Pacific Ocean. There, he made an important treaty with the local sultan, establishing a spice trade with the English. His triumphant return fuelled English ambitions to procure riches through the spice trade in the East.

The English East India Company was formed on 31 December 1600. At first united by conflict with Catholic Spain, the Dutch and British managed to avoid aggressive competition, but the harmony was short-lived. Deception and antagonism between Dutch and British traders came to a head in 1620 when the Dutch forced the British off the nutmeg-rich island of Run, the only one of the Spice Islands over which the British had complete control. Eventually they were forced to abandon the Spice Islands to concentrate on the pepper trade from India and later found a whole new route trading tea from China for Indian opium.

By 1663, the Dutch occupied Melaka, Cochin and much of Ceylon, and had a safe port in Cape Town. Amsterdam became one of the richest ports of the world and the Dutch-controlled Batavia (now Jakarta) became the Asian capital of the spice trade. The Dutch traders, set on winning huge profits, ruthlessly manipulated the markets for cloves, nutmeg and mace, sometimes burning tons of spices to force up prices. The wealth they acquired was spent at home. Huge tracts of land were reclaimed from the sea, and grand architecture and fine art flourished.

The Portuguese kept a small territory in East Timor but concentrated their Asian activities on Goa and Macao. Spain held the Philippines until 1898, when the islands became the first Asian colony of the United States of America. Britain kept control of Singapore and Malaysia, and France developed colonies in Indochina, both nations exploiting the land and people much as the Dutch did in Indonesia. Siam (Thailand) alone in Southeast Asia remained free of European colonists. As a result, Thai spices like lime leaves, galangal and lemon grass had much less of a role in the early spice trade than pepper, cloves and nutmeg. With the increasing popularity that Thai cuisine now enjoys around the world, however, these spices are becoming as widely traded as any.

# bangkok

As restaurateurs, we felt rather fraudulent as we entered the classroom, but we hadn't come to steal recipes; we were just keen to learn more about Thai cuisine. We had enrolled on the four-day course at the Thai Cooking School run by the Oriental Hotel in Bangkok. The Oriental promised to be a stylish base for a 'working' holiday.

The school was in an old colonial-style building with polished wooden floors, cream shutters and a wide veranda, among the tropical trees and palms on the opposite bank of the Chao Phraya. A ferry navigates its way between convoys of heavily laden barges, sluggish country rice boats and speeding 'long tail' river taxis. It's an entertaining way to go to school.

Our fellow students were three European women friends whose husbands were stationed in Bangkok, a honeymoon couple from California, a couple of English food lovers on their way to visit family in Australia and a lone Dutchman who was busy videotaping the classes while the rest of us scribbled notes. Our teacher was the skilled Mr Prem.

On our first day we learned how to make a herbed peanut sauce with crispy rice chips, deep-fried king prawn rolls, a herbed salad with winged beans and a chilli jam. Just as interesting were the tips we picked up about Thai ingredients, such as how to recognize and use all the many different types of noodle available, how to neutralize bitterness through combinations of spices and how to choose a good fish sauce. The best, we learned, is made solely from tiny anchovies which, despite a rather grim-sounding fermentation process, produce a flavour that is essential to authentic Thai cuisine. Cheaper versions may involve the decomposition of all kinds of marine life and can be unacceptably pungent to pampered stomachs. This explains the challenging nature of some dishes in parts of rural Thailand.

On subsequent days, we cooked spicy soups, creamy curries and delicious desserts. We steamed, stir fried and sautéed, and learned creative carving of fruit and vegetables. The course provided us with plenty of new recipes, which, with a little adaptation, we were able to cook in London. Any qualms about possible accusations of culinary espionage

*The colourful flower market on the banks of the Chao Phaya River in Bangkok.*

were soon put to rest when we chatted to the lone Dutchman with the video camera. Although he owned a restaurant and bar in the southern resort of Phuket, he had no personal interest in cooking and was only attending the course to record it as an instruction video for his cooks.

Afternoons and evenings were free, and as most of Bangkok's shops stay open late, quests for bargain antiques, jewellery, designer clothes and shoes or traditional silks could be conducted without wasting daylight. The most painless shopping is in the air-conditioned stores around Silom Road behind the hotel or in the multistorey River City complex. Better

*In the Bangkok temple of Wat Pho we found the the largest collection of antique Buddha images in Thailand. This graceful reclining Buddha was my favourite.*

## Galangal
### (*Alpinia galanga*)

Galangal is a type of ginger, a rhizome from Asia. Greater galangal is often used with lemon grass in Thai, Malaysian and Indonesian cooking. Lesser galangal is native to China, and is stronger. Like lemon grass and makrut lime leaves, galangal has only gained popularity in the West relatively recently.

## Lemon Grass
### (*Cymbopogum flexuosus*)

Lemon grass is a tropical grass of Southeast Asia. The stalks are used widely in the region for their aromatic citrus flavour, and the leaves make refreshingly invigorating citronella tea.

## Makrut Lime
### (*Citrus hystrix*)

The makrut lime tree is native to Southeast Asia and produces bitter fruits on stalks with distinctive pairs of leaves. The leaves are commonly used as a spice in Thai and Malaysian cooking, and some dishes also incorporate the zest of the fruit.

bargains and more fun are available at the Chatuchak, the huge weekend market in the north of the city. This is also a good place to buy ingredients to take home for cooking Thai recipes.

We were the only foreign tourists in the vast Buddha-image factories in the back streets around Phra Nakhon. There were Buddhas piled up in their hundreds, others being polished and film-wrapped, yet more lined up for collection. Some are so big they can only be shifted about by fork-lift trucks. Our long-boat trip into the labyrinth of Bangkok's canals or *klongs* was another interesting experience and much more exciting that the rather contrived floating market tour. The *klongs* soon leave the city in a direction too wet for roads and give a glimpse of a more traditional life among wooden houses built on stilts in an attractive version of suburbia.

## TOM KHA GAI

*This soup has the quintessential taste of Thailand: a simple combination of galangal, lemon grass, lime leaves, chopped coriander and chillies that fills the mouth with fresh and exciting sensations.*

SERVES 4

500ml/16fl oz coconut milk
4cm/1¼ in piece galangal root, cut into thin slices
3 lemon grass stalks, bashed with a rolling pin, and cut into 2.5cm/1in pieces
8 lime leaves, torn in half
300g/10oz skinless chicken breast, sliced

90g/3oz shiitake mushrooms, cut into quarters
3 tablespoons fish sauce
1½ tablespoons brown sugar
4 tablespoons lime juice
handful of coriander leaves, chopped
3 red chillies, thinly sliced

In a saucepan, heat half of the coconut milk with 350ml/12fl oz of water, together with the galangal, lemon grass and lime leaves. When the milk starts to boil, add the chicken, mushrooms, fish sauce and sugar, cover the pan and simmer gently until the chicken is tender and cooked through. Add the remaining coconut milk and 50ml/2fl oz of water, bring back to the boil, and remove from heat.

Place 1 tablespoon of lime juice in the bottom of each bowl and pour the soup over the top. Serve garnished with coriander leaves and sliced fresh chilli.

## HERBED GREEN BEAN SALAD

*This salad makes a good starter in its own right. The ingredients combine to create a wonderful mixture of tastes.*

SERVES 4–6

90g/3oz peanuts, skinned
115g/4oz fresh coconut meat, finely
  sliced (see page 60)
115g/4oz deep-fried tofu, sliced
2 tablespoons brown sugar
2 tablespoons fish sauce
4 tablespoons lime juice
300g/10oz flat green beans, blanched
  and thinly sliced
150g/5oz bean sprouts

175g/6oz cooked small prawns,
  chopped in half
8 shallots, thinly sliced
2 red chillies, thinly sliced
8 lime leaves, thinly sliced
2 lemon grass stalks, thinly sliced
handful of basil leaves, roughly
  chopped
handful of coriander leaves

In a small pan, dry-roast the peanuts until they turn golden brown. Remove them from the heat and grind them until finely chopped. Then, in the same pan, gently dry-roast the coconut meat until it is golden brown. Remove it from the heat and set it to one side. Still using the same pan, toast the deep-fried tofu until it is brown on both sides.

In a large bowl, make the salad dressing by combining the brown sugar with the fish sauce and the lime juice. Then add the blanched green beans, the bean sprouts, the cooked prawns, the shallots, the chillies, the lime leaves, the lemon grass, the basil leaves and the ground peanuts. Mix all the ingredients well.

Serve piled in the centre of a plate garnished with the tofu slices, the roasted coconut slices and the coriander leaves.

*Herbed green bean salad*

# lombok

Lombok lies among the group of Indonesian islands to the east of Java and was colonized by the Balinese from the early seventeenth century until 1894. Their influence was always strongest in the west where there are still many remains of their rule, including temples and a water palace, as well as a sizeable Balinese population. 'Local dishes' on hotel and café menus are almost always Balinese.

Most people on Lombok are Sasaks, descendants of early migrants from a part of Asia near Burma. Although diluted by conversions to Islam, by Balinese and Dutch colonialism, and more recently by the centralized rule of Jakarta, Sasak culture still gives Lombok a unique feel. Unlike the public spectacles of Bali, traditional rituals of marriage and death are still largely private affairs. There are many villages where life seems to continue much as it must have done for centuries, people speak only the complicated Sasak language and are simply occupied in subsistence farming and fishing: using oxen to cultivate rice and vegetables on the fertile slopes of Mount Rinjani or setting out to sea in their elegant, brightly painted outrigger *prahu* boats. Lombok is a very beautiful island, with fields of vivid green divided by rows of swaying palm trees, miles of deserted white sandy beaches and plenty of timeless rural charm.

The word 'lombok' in Bahasa Indonesian means chilli. Use of it in island cookery is widespread. Although cafés are scarce in the villages, we did find fiery Sasak food in Lombok's capital, Matram, where we were recommended a restaurant called Dua Em. We sat on the floor at a low table on a bamboo veranda overlooking a courtyard full of tropical vegetation: a seductive setting for some unusual dishes. I enjoyed the *kelor* – a clear soup of a water spinach leaf called *kangkung* which was clean and peppery. The main course of chicken fried with banana pith, coconut juice, garlic and a very hot chilli sauce called *bumbu* was delicious. The accompanying side dish of pea aubergines in a pungent *plecing* sauce was scarier; the strong fishy taste was a bit too jungly for me.

Out on the road there were no restaurants or petrol stations (we had to buy petrol for our jeep out of jerrycans on the side of the road). However, we did find one of the most special hotels of our travels. At the

*Girls selling pineapples on the beach on Lombok.*

Lombok Oberoi we experienced designer luxury at its zenith. The Balinese menu was excellent and so was the two-hour *lulur* treatment, promoted as one for honeymooners. It includes a full body scrub with aromatic pastes, being covered from head to foot in cold yoghurt, bathed in a warm pool filled with jasmine, frangipani and ylang-ylang petals and more deep massage. Throughout all this we were obliged to wear some comical disposable underpants. Sitting on a bed covered in yoghurt in a pair of paper pants would certainly be a novel way to start married life.

## SPICY INDONESIAN PRAWNS

SERVES 4

| | |
|---|---|
| 3 tablespoons sunflower oil | 2.5cm/1in piece of galangal, peeled |
| 1 red onion, thinly sliced | and grated |
| 2 garlic cloves, crushed | 175ml/6fl oz coconut milk |
| 3 red chillies, thinly sliced | 1 teaspoon tamarind paste |
| 450g/1lb prawns | 1/2 teaspoon black pepper, freshly |
| 1/2 teaspoon chilli flakes | ground |
| 1/2 teaspoon ground turmeric | bunch of spring onions, thinly sliced |
| 2 medium tomatoes, cut into small | salt to taste |
| cubes | 6oz/175g bean sprouts |
| 2 lemon grass stalks, thinly sliced | handful of coriander leaves, chopped |

In a wok, heat the sunflower oil and fry the onion, garlic and chopped red chillies until soft. Add the prawns and fry them until tender. Add the chilli flakes and turmeric and fry for 30 seconds; then add the cubed tomatoes and fry for 3 minutes, stirring constantly. Add the lemon grass and galangal and fry for another 30 seconds.

Pour in the coconut milk and tamarind paste dissolved in 60ml/2fl oz of warm water. Sprinkle over the black pepper and simmer gently for 3 minutes. Add the spring onions and salt to taste.

Serve garnished with a mound of bean sprouts sprinkled with the chopped coriander.

### Cloves
### (*Syzyium aromaticum*)

Like nutmeg and mace, cloves are native to just a few remote islands among the Moluccas of Indonesia and have been one of the most traded spices in history. First Asian, then Portuguese, Dutch, French, British and Arab traders dominated the clove trade.

The spice is a dried flower with an unmistakable sweet and pungent fragrance. It is used in both sweet and savoury dishes and is an essential ingredient of Indian garam masala, the French *quatre épices* and Chinese five spice mix.

Zanzibar has taken over as the world's main producer of cloves, although much of the crop finds its way back to Indonesia for the manufacture of kretek clove oil cigarettes. The oil is also used as a preservative and as an antiseptic in dental medicine.

*Spicy Indonesian prawns*

## INDONESIAN SATAY BARBECUE

*This combination of marinade and sauce can be used with anything from vegetables and tofu to chicken and meat or fish. Marinade 1kg/2lb of your chosen ingredients while the sauce is being made, then barbecue them.*

SERVES 4–6

### For the marinade

1 dessertspoon coriander seeds
½ teaspoon turmeric powder
3 garlic cloves, roughly chopped
2 red chillies, roughly chopped
5cm/2in piece of ginger, roughly
   chopped
1 stalk of lemon grass, thinly sliced
4cm/1½ in piece of jaggery or
   1 dessertspoon brown sugar)
handful of coriander leaves, chopped
juice of a lime
2 tablespoons sunflower oil

### For the satay sauce

175g/6oz peanuts, skinned
2 teaspoons coriander seeds

1 teaspoon fennel seeds
1 teaspoon cumin seeds
4 red chillies, roughly chopped
2 lemon grass sticks, finely chopped
5 shallots, peeled and roughly
   chopped
2 garlic cloves, roughly chopped
1 teaspoon dried shrimp paste
8 candlenuts or macadamia nuts or
   cashew nuts
1 teaspoon tamarind purée
2 tablespoons sunflower oil
175ml/6fl oz coconut milk
2 tablespoons light soya sauce
8cm/3in piece jaggery or 1
   tablespoon brown sugar
salt to taste

Start by making the marinade. Dry-roast the coriander seeds in a small pan until they are aromatic, remove from the heat and grind to a powder. Place in a blender with all the remaining marinade ingredients and blend until smooth. Cover 1kg/2lb of your barbecue ingredients and leave for 1 hour.

Then make the satay sauce. In a small frying pan, dry-roast the peanuts gently until they begin to brown, remove from the heat, and grind until finely chopped. Dry-roast the coriander, fennel and cumin seeds until they are aromatic, remove from the heat and grind to a powder. Place in a blender with the chillies, lemon grass, shallots, garlic, shrimp paste and candlenuts. Blend to a paste.

Dissolve the tamarind in the boiling water, and set to one side. In a saucepan, heat the oil and fry the spice paste for 1 minute, stirring constantly. Stir in the ground peanuts. Add the tamarind water, coconut milk, soya sauce and jaggery, stir until combined, bring to the boil, then cover the pan and simmer gently, stirring regularly until the oil returns and the sauce reduces. Add salt to taste.

When your chosen ingredients have marinaded, thread them on to skewers and barbecue them. Serve sizzling hot with plenty of satay sauce.

**The ubiquitous chilli is used extensively in Indonesian cuisine.**

# the strait of malacca

The settlements at either end of the Strait of Malacca have both played an important role in the history of the Asian spice routes. At the northern end is Malacca itself, now known as Melaka, which was once the most strategically important port in the international spice trade between east and west. Today it is a small provincial town of little significance to the rest of the world. At the southern end is Singapore, a pirate- and malaria-infested swamp town during Malacca's heyday, which is now one of the most powerful and wealthy ports in the world.

The Strait offers the fastest sea route between the South China Sea and the Indian Ocean. Early spice traders from China, India, Siam and Indonesia all used it as a regular route between sources and markets. The port stood conveniently halfway between China and India, and the Strait linked the Spice Islands with the Malabar Coast of India.

Malacca was more than just a wealthy port. Founded in 1400 by the Sumatran Hindu prince Paramesvara, it became a powerful trading state and home to a large expatriate Chinese community. Islam came to Malacca from the Middle East, via Gujarati spice merchants, and the port was soon the centre of Islam in Southeast Asia.

Afonso d'Albuquerque's Portuguese fleet sailed into the Strait in 1511, seeking the first European trade route to the sources of nutmeg and cloves. Malacca was conquered and occupied by Portugal for a hundred years. The Portuguese language was established among the resulting Eurasian population, but attempts to spread Catholicism mostly failed and led to a boycott of Malacca by Muslim sailors. The decline in Malacca's importance was reversed when the Protestant Dutch ousted the Portuguese and concentrated on incorporating the port into their Southeast Asian empire.

During the Napoleonic Wars in Europe, Britain stepped in to protect the Dutch territories from French occupation. Following the French defeat, the British, not wanting a return to Dutch domination of the spice trade in the region, negotiated the ceding of Malacca to their own crown. The key player in these 1824 negotiations was Sir Stamford Raffles, who had established a free port on the island of Singapore the previous year, giving Britain control of both ends of the Strait. Malacca and Singapore, together with Penang to the north, became known as the Straits Settlements. They became key ports in the British trade of Indian opium to China and Chinese tea to Europe. Penang and Singapore attracted huge

*The Strait at sunset. These waters are the gateway to the Far East.*

migrant populations of Cantonese and Hakkas from China and Tamils from India, but Malacca was soon the least significant of the three ports.

Singapore's boom followed the opening of the Suez Canal in 1869, when it became an important stopover between London and the Far East. By the time Singapore was declared an independent country in 1965, the expatriate Chinese dominated Singapore, bringing their cuisine and spices with them. Singapore remained a free port and prospered, and by the 1970s it was the richest country in Asia after Japan.

*Architecture in Melaka today is similar to that of Singapore, dominated by high-rise glass, steel and concrete. The old town, however, still has remnants of a more colourful past, including the Dutch church.*

Eating out is a serious part of daily life. The easiest and cheapest way to enjoy Chinese food is at one of the Hawkers' Centres, where dozens of stalls provide steaming dishes of fresh food with a flurry of chopping and sizzling woks.

Today, old Melaka is a romantic and atmospheric enclave of crumbling colonial Dutch and Portuguese churches and streets of migrant Chinese merchant houses. We found the 'devil's curry' featured below in a café along Medan Portugis.

## MELAKAN DEVIL'S MUSHROOM CURRY

*This recipe has a sixteenth-century Portuguese origin. Aubergines, Asian mushrooms and water chestnuts are combined with Indian and Southeast Asian spices to produce a robust dish which also works well with meat.*

### SERVES 4

4 tablespoons sunflower oil

1 heaped teaspoon black mustard seeds

1 heaped teaspoon fenugreek seeds

2 large red onions, finely chopped

3 garlic cloves, finely chopped

5cm/2in piece of ginger, cut into strips

6 red chillies, finely sliced

225g/8oz baby aubergines, cut in half lengthwise

salt

200g/7oz shiitake mushrooms, cut into quarters

200g/7oz oyster mushrooms, thickly sliced

115g/4oz water chestnuts

8 ground candlenuts or macadamia nuts or cashew nuts

1 teaspoon ground turmeric

2.5cm/1in piece galangal, grated

2 lemon grass stalks, finely sliced

1 teaspoon dried shrimp paste

300ml/10fl oz vegetable stock

1 tablespoon dark soya sauce

175g/6oz bean sprouts

handful of coriander leaves, chopped

**Mace is the red cage that encases the nutmeg kernel. It is native to just a few islands of Indonesia.**

In a large saucepan, heat the oil and add the mustard and fenugreek seeds. When they crackle, add the onion, garlic, ginger and chillies, and fry until they start to soften. Add the baby aubergine, sprinkle with a litle salt to prevent from drying, and fry until golden brown, stirring regularly.

Add the shiitake and oyster mushrooms and fry for a further few minutes. Add the water chestnuts. ground candlenuts, turmeric, grated galangal, lemon grass and shrimp paste, and fry for 30 seconds, stiring well. Add the vegetable stock and soya sauce, and bring to the boil. Cover the pan and simmer gently for 10 minutes, with salt to taste.

Serve garnished with bean sprouts and coriander leaves.

## CHINESE FIVE-SPICE

*The traditional blend of spices known as Chinese five-spice is found in every China Town in the world. This recipe makes enough for the fish dish below.*

| | |
|---|---|
| ¹/₂ teaspoon fennel | ¹/₂ teaspoon sichuan pepper |
| 1 star anise | ¹/₂ teaspoon cloves |
| 1.5cm/¹/₂in piece of cinnamon stick | |

In a small frying pan dry-roast the spices until aromatic, remove them from heat and grind to a powder.

## FISH COOKED WITH CHINESE FIVE-SPICE

*We ate this at a street stall food emporium in Singapore, the largest China Town anywhere outside China.*

SERVES 4

| | |
|---|---|
| 1¹/₂ tablespoons dark soya sauce | 4 175g/6oz fillets of red mullet or |
| 3 tablespoons light soya sauce | other white fish |
| 1¹/₂ tablespoons Chinese rice wine | 45g/1¹/₂oz brown sugar |
| 4cm/1¹/₂in piece of ginger, peeled and | Chinese five-spice (see above) |
| grated | 4 tablespoons sunflower oil |
| 3 garlic cloves, finely chopped | 225g/8oz spinach leaves |
| 8 spring onions, sliced | 1 tablespoon sesame seeds |

Combine the dark and light soya sauce, the rice wine, ginger, garlic and spring onion, pour over the fish fillets and leave to marinade for 1 hour.

Dissolve the brown sugar in 250ml/8fl oz of hot water, and add the Chinese five-spice.

In a large wok or frying pan, heat the oil and fry the fish along with any of the marinade left in the bowl, until golden brown on both sides. Pour in the sugar and the Chinese five-spice mixture and simmer gently for 3 minutes.

Wilt the spinach in boiling water, remove from the heat and drain well. In a small frying pan, dry-roast the sesame seeds until they start to pop, then remove from the heat.

Serve the fish on a bed of spinach sprinkled with sesame seeds. Spoon the sauce over the top and serve immediately.

**Star Anise
(*Illicium verum*)**
The most beautiful of spices, star anise is an eight-pointed star with sweet liquorice-flavoured seeds housed in its carpels. It is native to the hills of southwest China and is used extensively in Chinese and Vietnamese cooking. In Europe it was not so easy to trade as it shares a flavour with the unrelated anise, which grows locally.

**Sichuan Pepper
(*Zanthoxylum piperitum*)**
Despite a long history as a staple spice of the Sichuan region of China, these dried berries have not been widely traded or used outside the Chinese community except in Japan. Their prevalence in Sichuan cooking has given it the reputation of being the hottest style of Chinese cooking, although the effect is more woody and numbing than burning.

**Cassia Bark
(*Cinnamomum cassia*)**
The trees that yield cassia bark are native to the jungle hills around the border of China and Burma. The spice resembles the bark of cinnamon trees that grow in Sri Lanka but is considered inferior. Cassia followed the earliest spice routes out of China so has a long history of use as far away as Arabia and the eastern Mediterranean.

*Fish cooked with Chinese five-spice*

the americas

ABOVE: *Part of one of the murals by Diego Rivera on the walls of the Palacio Nacional in Mexico City, illustrating trade in a pre-Columbian Mexico town.*

PAGES 120–21: *The Pan-American Highway winding its way north along the Pacific coast of Peru through a land permanently shrouded in mists where the hot desert meets the cold ocean.*

The civilizations of Central and South America have a long history. In Mexico, the Olmecs in Tabasco, the Zapotecs of Oaxaca, the Izapa of Chiapas, the pyramid builders of Teotihuacán and the mighty Mayans of the Yucatan had all come and gone by the time Europeans encountered the Aztecs living there at the beginning of the sixteenth century. The Inca civilization that Europeans came across in Peru a few years later had been preceded by those of the Chimú, the Tiahuanaco, the Moche, the Nazca and the Chavin.

Like others before them, both Aztec and Inca empires grew weak through over-expansion. Meanwhile, the merchants of Venice and Cairo and countless middlemen along the established spice routes between Asia and Europe were about to become victims of their own success. The ever-increasing demand from the tables of Europe's rich for exotic flavourings were inflating prices, but by the end of the fifteenth century navigation skills and ships had improved and cartographers were speculating on new routes to break the Venetian–Mameluke monopoly.

Portuguese explorers sailed south along the coast of Africa until they found their way around the Cape of Good Hope into the Indian Ocean and later east to India. In 1492, an Italian merchant seaman named Christopher Columbus, who had settled in Portugal as a mapmaker, persuaded Queen Isabella of Spain to support a speculative westward expedition to look for an even faster route to the spice lands of Asia.

When Columbus reached land, probably one of the Bahamas, he was convinced he was off the coast of India or China and that the islanders were Indians. He sailed on to Cuba and Haiti, finding plenty of exotic produce, but not the pepper he was seeking. Assuming that the source of spices must be close, Isabella sponsored three more expeditions led by Columbus across the Atlantic, during which he visited much of the Caribbean and returned with chillies and allspice, new and exciting spices but still not the essential pepper.

At the time of his death in 1506, Columbus was completely unaware of the significance of his discoveries. Asserting that he had been lost somewhere in Asia, he had not even named the lands he had found. This was left to another Italian navigator, Amerigo Vespucci, who realized that these lands were not Asia but a 'New World'. The maps were redrawn and the 'new' lands named after Vespucci.

The Americas soon became a focus of attention for Spanish and Portuguese. Ferdinand Magellan, a Portuguese sailor working for the King of Spain, was the first to navigate around the continent and on across the

Pacific. He reached the Philippines, laying the foundations for a Spanish colony in Asia, and proved there was a westward route to Asia, even if it was a lot longer than had been imagined. Although he was killed in the Philippines, his one remaining ship was taken safely back to Spain, thus completing the very first circumnavigation of the globe.

The voyages of discovery to the east by the Portuguese had provided Europe with a huge increase in trade of goods that were already comparatively well known. Voyages to the west, however, brought back cargoes of completely new products that were to have lasting effects on international cuisine. Chillies and allspice were just the beginning. In addition, European kitchens were introduced to tomatoes, vanilla, avocados, peanuts, potatoes, sweet peppers, maize, cocoa, squashes and new types of beans. People began to ruin their health by smoking tobacco, and lives

*Multicoloured cobs of corn in a market in the Sacred Valley of the Incas, Peru.*

were saved as quinine became the first available protection to travellers against malaria. Coca was used as a new anaesthetic. None of these though, had as much of an attraction to the Spanish explorers as rumours of unimaginable pots of gold and silver.

The first Spaniards the Aztecs encountered were not spice merchants but gold-hungry conquistadors. In 1519 Hernàn Cortés landed in Mexico with six hundred men, a few cannons and horses and some nasty diseases. In only two years, helped by disaffected tribes and a lack of resistance to European disease among the Aztecs, he and his men had defeated the empire and destroyed the Aztec capital of Tenochtitlán, where Mexico City stands today.

The Incas had controlled a vast empire boasting architectural triumphs and sophisticated systems of agriculture, communication and society, all achieved without use of the wheel, writing, iron, draught animals, the arch or mortar. It existed in isolation from the outside world until the sixteenth century, when the Spanish conquistador Francisco Pizarro landed on the Peruvian coast. By putting to death the Incan emperor Atahuallpa at a time when the empire was already weakened by civil war, Pizarro and his small band of followers found conquest easy. During the years of the Inquisition Inca culture was almost wiped out.

Despite having been the first parts of America visited by Europeans, the islands of the Caribbean took longer to become colonies of Europe. The Carib people, who had stolen the islands from peaceful and sophisticated Arawaks around 1200 AD, proved a more formidable foe than either Aztecs or Incas. Eventually, however, each of the Caribbean islands was made the property of a European power. Land was cleared for commercial plantations of imported crops like sugar and bananas and slaves were brought from Africa to work them. Jamaica remains the world's main supplier of allspice – Grenada grows a third of the world's nutmeg, introduced by the British to break the Dutch monopoly of the spice in the Banda Islands of the East Indies.

*A statue of Christ looks down over the colonial Spanish city of Cuzco from the ruins of Sacsyhuaman – once a great temple to the Sun God of the Incas. Stones from Inca buildings were used in the construction of the churches and palaces of the conquistadors.*

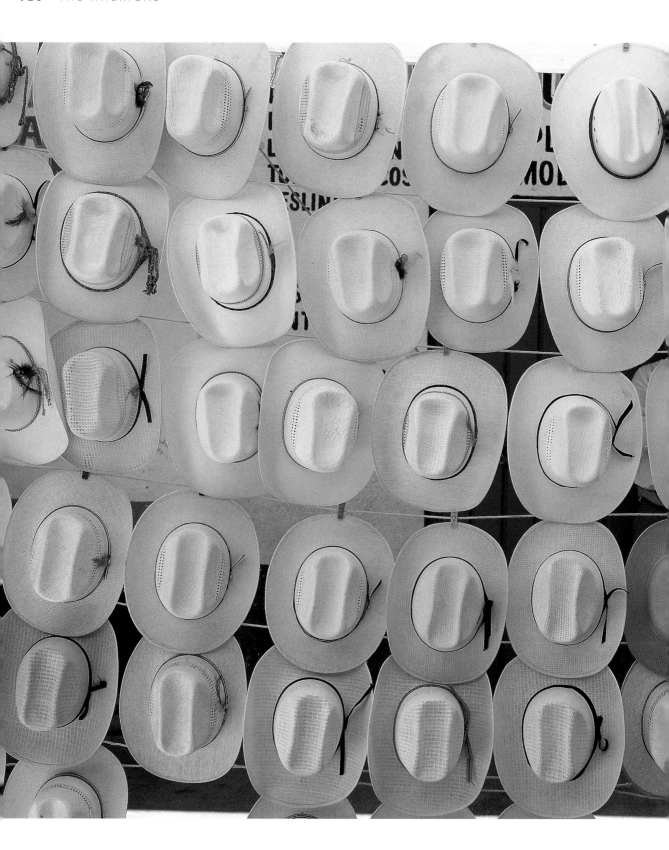

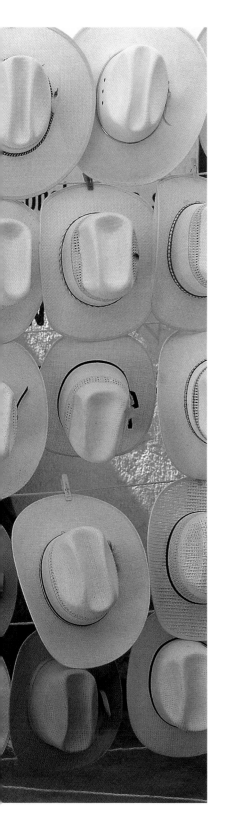

# mexico

The cuisine of modern Mexico is dominated by indigenous ingredients. Hundreds of chilli varieties provide a great range of colours, tastes and shapes, and are included in almost every Mexican meal, either as a main ingredient or in a salsa. They come stuffed, fresh, dried, sliced as a garnish, fried in batter, smoked and pickled. Some are ferocious and others so tame they are sweet; not all Mexican food need be hot but some is, extremely. The tomato is also ubiquitous, both as the main ingredient of the salsas that accompany every meal and as a common component of soups, stews and salads.

Corn (maize) is the daily staple, soaked, dried and ground into flour to make toasted tortillas; wrapped, as a dough mixed with spices and meat or vegetables, in a banana leaf and steamed as tamales; fried into corn chips, or sometimes just eaten off the cob. Beans are boiled and mashed then fried with spices to make refries. Avocados are puréed into guacamole, chocolate melted into mole sauce and peanuts ground into butter. Vanilla and pecan nuts are baked into pies and puddings.

Many of Mexico's earliest European settlers were Andalucians from southern Spain, and many of the imported ingredients used are a legacy of the Arab Moors' 700-year residence in that area. Rice is served steamed as a side dish or mixed with beans. Limes make regular appearances in salsas as well as in guacamole and in one of Mexico's favourite drinks, margarita. Olives, olive oil, oregano, saffron, garlic and cheese are also found in Mexican recipes. Coriander, originally from the eastern Mediterranean, has become the most used spice after chilli, finding its way into salsas, soups and stews. Cheese became popular with the introduction of Spanish domestic cattle. *Queso anejo* resembles parmesan, and a stringy style of cheese made in Oaxaca is similar to mozzarella.

Mexicans love to eat out and cities are full of cafés and restaurants serving fine food, often with live musicians. Main plazas are usually lined with alfresco eating places and there is always plenty of cheap and often good street food down the alleys.

There are lots of regional variations in Mexican cooking, so travelling round the country is never dull in terms of eating out. Two of the best

**Straw hats in a Oaxaca market.**

**The unusual fruit of the cashew tree
has a very short shelf life, so it needs
to be eaten the day it is picked. The
tree is more famous for its nuts, which
like the chilli have been exported
from the Americas to every corner
of the planet.**

dishes we discovered were the nutty stuffed chillies *en nogada* —
freshened with tangy pomegranate seeds — from the cool colonial hill
town of Puebla, and a barbecue of marinaded giant Caribbean prawns
with a spicy orange, coriander and olive sauce which we had on the steamy
Yucatan coast.

## CHILLIES EN NOGADA

*This recipe is traditionally associated with the Central Mexican city of Puebla,
although versions of it turn up all over Latin America. Fist-sized mild green
poblano peppers are ideal for stuffing, but any good-sized red or green pepper
is suitable. The stuffing is a delicious creamy, nutty, spicy concoction, finished off
perfectly by the pomegranate seeds.*

SERVES 4

8 poblano peppers or similar
2 tablespoons sunflower oil
1 large onion, finely chopped
2 garlic cloves, finely chopped
1 jalapeño chilli, finely chopped
30g/1oz almonds, finely chopped
60g/2oz walnuts, finely chopped
75g/2½ oz raisins

2 celery sticks, cut into small cubes
4 medium tomatoes, cut into small
  cubes
salt and ground black pepper
250ml/16fl oz double cream
4 tablespoons flat-leaf parsley,
  chopped
seeds of a pomegranate

Remove the skins from the poblano peppers. To do this, roast them under
a hot grill, turning frequently, until the skins blister. Place in a bowl and cover
with clingfilm for 5 minutes. The skins should then peel off easily. Slice the
peppers down one side and remove the seeds and veins.

Make the stuffing in a frying pan. Heat the oil and fry the onion, garlic
and jalapeño chilli until soft and golden. Add the chopped nuts and the
raisins and fry for 1 minute, then add the celery and fry for another 2
minutes. Add the chopped tomato, half a teaspoon of black pepper and salt
to taste. Gently cook until the moisture of the tomatoes has been
absorbed.

Stuff the peppers with the nutty mixture and place in a heatproof dish.
Combine the cream with 75ml/2½fl oz of water, the parsley, salt and black
pepper to taste, and pour over the stuffed peppers.

Grill the peppers until the cream is hot and the peppers are browned.
Serve sprinkled with the pomegranate seeds.

**Chillies en nogada**

## YUCATAN RECADO MARINADE

*This combination of marinade and sauce typical of Mexico's Yucatan Peninsula can be used with anything from vegetables and tofu to chicken and meat or fish. The ingredients of choice can be marinaded while the sauce is being made then cooked on a barbecue or grill and served sizzling hot with plenty of the spicy orange and olive sauce.*

### SERVES 4–6

2 medium red onions, sliced
6 garlic cloves with skins on
9 whole allspice seeds
10 cloves
2.5cm/1in piece of cinnamon stick
1½ teaspoons cumin seeds
1½ teaspoons coriander seeds
4 tablespoons olive oil

juice of 2 limes
1 habañero chilli, seeded and roughly
  chopped
2 teaspoons dried oregano
1 teaspoon salt
1 heaped teaspoon ground black
  pepper

Under a pre-heated grill, roast the onion and garlic until brown and set to one side. In a small pan, dry-roast the whole spices until aromatic and grind to a powder. Place in a food processor with the onion, garlic, olive oil, lime juice, chilli, oregano, salt and black pepper. Blend until smooth.

Coat the chosen ingredients with half the blended marinade and leave for 1 hour. Keep the other half for use in the recado sauce recipe, right.

**Red chillies.**

### Chilli
### (*Capsicum* spp.)

Despite being the most recent spice to join international spice routes, chilli has become the superlative spice. Chillies are all originally native to Mexico and were cultivated more than six thousand years before Columbus arrived in the Caribbean looking for Indian pepper. Many different cultivars of chilli developed in different conditions, giving a huge variety of colours, size and strength. The Spanish and Portuguese introduced them to India and Southeast Asia in the sixteenth century and the popularity of chillies spread rapidly across the globe.

Today, chilli is the most cultivated spice in the world, with hundreds of varieties available. The hottest varieties tend to grow in the tropics and milder ones in temperate climates. Some of the hottest varieties are the Mexican 'Habañero', the Caribbean 'Early Scotch Bonnet', the Thai 'Bird's Eye', and the Indonesian 'Lombok'. A new cultivar has recently been developed in India that is so much hotter than all of these that its main use is in anti-attack pepper sprays.

The effect when eaten is to stimulate the palate, aid digestion, increase blood circulation and cause perspiration. This has a cooling effect on the body, which may be one reason why hotter chillies are popular in countries with tropical climates. However, many people – and not just in hot countries – derive an almost euphoric pleasure from eating the hottest chillies in their food. There is a theory that the brain releases endorphins to combat the irritation of hot chilli in the mouth and stomach and that these induce mild states of euphoria. Once 'addicted' to the pleasure of chilli, larger quantities are needed to repeat the sensation. Strangely, however, it is by no means a universal passion and other people find the sensation thoroughly disagreeable.

Paprika is a mild capsicum that is dried and made into a powder with the seeds and membranes removed. It is popular in Hungary and most cuisines around the Mediterranean. Cayenne is another chilli used as a powder. It is considerably hotter when seeds and membrane are included .

**Vanilla**
**(*Vanilla planifolia*)**
Vanilla is a tropical orchid native to Mexico. Sun-dried for several months, the pod and tiny fragrant seeds produce an exotic and intense flavour that is now popular all over the world.

Early attempts to grow vanilla away from Mexico as a commercial spice failed, as pollination relies exclusively on a single species of hummingbird or on melipona bees, both of which are unique to Mexico. All vanilla had to be shipped from its source until the nineteenth century, when French botanists developed artificial methods of pollination on Indian Ocean islands. Today, Madagascar is a major producer, with smaller industries in the Comoro Islands, Réunion and the Seychelles.

Pure vanilla extract can be used instead of fresh pods, but avoid synthetic chemical substitutes.

## YUCATAN RECADO SAUCE

SERVES 4–6

2 red peppers
1 yellow pepper
3 tablespoons olive oil
recado marinade (see left)
1lb/450g plum tomatoes, pulped in a
    blender until smooth

zest and juice of a large orange
about 30 green olives
2 handfuls of coriander leaves,
    chopped
ground black pepper and salt to taste

First remove the skins from the peppers. Roast them under a pre-heated grill, turning frequently, until blackened on all sides, then place them in a bowl, cover in clingfilm and leave for 5 minutes. The skins should peel away easily. Cut the peppers in half and remove the seeds and stalks, then thinly slice. Set to one side.

In a large frying pan, heat the oil and add the recado marinade, stirring constantly for 1 minute. Pour on the pulped tomatoes and simmer gently for 5 minutes. Next, add the peppers, orange zest and juice, olives and coriander, and simmer until the sauce reduces and the oil returns. Add black pepper and salt to taste.

Barbecue or grill the chosen ingredients and serve with the sauce on the side.

*Green chillies.*

# peru

In February 1986 I achieved a lifetime ambition: climbing the precipitous stairway of stones carved out of the Peruvian jungle to Intipunku (the Gateway of the Sun), I had my first sight of Machu Picchu, the Lost City of the Incas. Its dramatic ruins are perched on a sheer-sided hilltop, surrounded by mighty Andean peaks immersed in swirling mists, with the Urubamba River roaring deep in the gorge below in its violent rush down to the Amazon. I was quite alone. Machu Picchu appeared to be as deserted as the day its Inca inhabitants mysteriously abandoned it to the jungle five hundred years ago.

This impressive memory is somewhat clouded by others more bleak and frightening of travelling in Peru at that time. The guerrillas of *Sendero Luminoso* (the Shining Path) had activated enough support to hold the country to ransom. Roads between cities were too dangerous to travel and the train to Machu Picchu had been blown up. Peru was a land of curfews and atrocities, fear and suspicion, and even tourists were declared targets for assassination. To make matters worse, my friend Robert and I had naively assumed that mid-summer would be a good time to trek the Andes. It is in fact the height of the rainy season. That first sight of Machu Picchu was one of tired relief as much as awesome wonder: the end of five long days on the Inca trail, dragging a heavy rucksack over 4,000m/13,000ft passes, camping in cold drizzle and living in soggy clothes on a diet of cold food.

I returned to Peru in May 1999 to trek a newly opened, shorter and easier Inca trail to Machu Picchu. Tempted by the promise of trekking in good weather and relative luxury, with guides, porters and cooks, I was also excited to be returning to a stable and safe Peru, but most of all by the prospect of seeing Machu Picchu again. I was not disappointed.

We flew to Cuzco, a beautiful mountain town with an ugly and cruel history, high in the Andes. It is a gem of Spanish colonial architecture, with cobbled streets and grand plazas, built by the conquistadors among the ruins of the Inca capital. To the Incas, Cuzco was the navel of the known world: the administrative, cultural and royal capital of a vast empire stretching down the spine of the Andes, westwards into the coastal deserts and eastwards into the jungles of the Amazon basin.

American Indian culture has proved most resistant to Spanish

*In a natural depression in the Andes at Moray are the remains of an Inca experimental agricultural project. Different crops were planted on the terraced fields to determine their optimum growing altitude.*

influence in the high Andes where the native population has survived in the greatest numbers. The Inca word for chilli, *aji*, is still in everyday use among the Quechua-speaking campasinos of the area. Dishes such as *papa a la huancaina*, which consists of boiled yellow-fleshed potatoes, and cobs of maize served with hard-boiled eggs and olives in a spicy cheese, cream and chilli sauce, are typical of pre-Columbian cookery.

Another dish that has endured with visible popularity in the Andes is *cuy*, or guinea pig. These are often roasted over charcoal or served in a stew with potatoes and flavoured with garlic and *aji*. We found a Cuzco restaurant that has made a speciality of serving whole roast guinea pig. Each oven-fresh animal is served standing bolt upright in a bed of salad and boiled potatoes, wearing a sombrero made of a halved tomato, carrying a miniature carrot walking stick and smoking a chilli cigar.

Breathing in Cuzco is literally a case of catching your breath. The air is alarmingly thin. Oxygen was available on room service at the hotel, from heavy iron cylinders. In the lobby, coca tea, a traditional antidote to the ill-effects of altitude, was available on tap.

Leaving Cuzco, we descended deep into the Urubamba Valley where

*The Quechua descendents of the Incas dominate the population of Andean Peru. Many are still farmers and live a traditional life. Peru's massive recent rise in popularity as a tourist destination, though, is attracting many to jobs as porters. Aided by constant consumption of coca leaves, they manage huge loads and still arrive at camps hours before their trekkers.*

it would be easier to acclimatize and our journey to Machu Picchu, first by road and then on foot, would begin. The Inca armies fled this way in the fifteenth century, carrying their gold – never found – with them. Before the walking started we visited the extensive ruins at Pisac, climbing the terraced hillsides above the village square where Quechua women sold vegetables, grains and spicy snacks under the shade of a giant tree hanging with cobweb moss. In Moray we saw the concentric terraces of an Inca experimental agricultural station descending the sides of a massive crater. In the village bars here, run by inebriated Quechua women in top hats, we tried the homemade beer, a fermented gruel which tasted like yoghurty cider. At Ollantaytambo, where the road ends and the trail begins, there are yet more impressive ruins, and a brisk trade in coca leaves. Chewed at length with lime or banana leaf ash, the leaves induce a feeling of well-being which alleviates the discomforts induced by altitude, fatigue and hunger. They are very popular with porters and backpackers.

After the first morning of walking, we saw no other trekkers. Stone Inca sentry posts covered in creepers confirmed the antiquity of the trail. Sometimes we walked next to the river, somtimes climbed high above it on spurs of the mountains that towered above us, their snowy peaks glinting in the bright sunshine. Rocky hillsides dotted with cacti gave way to landscapes reminiscent of the Scottish Highlands, then shaded forests of eucalyptus. We shared the trail with local farmers and their animals, and groups of children on their long hike to or from distant schools.

Our porters not only carried all our luggage, but sped on ahead of us to set up camp and prepare great meals (including *papa a la huancaina*). After lunch on the second day, the trail became sub-tropical, with buttress roots, hanging creepers, scarlet begonias and yellow orchids lining the jungle path. A trail warden called Felicito walked with us, plucking fresh passion fruits from the trees for us along the way. He told us how his dog had been eaten by a puma the previous day. None of us saw a puma, but we did see some panda-like spectacle bears, a snake and plenty of butter-flies and birds.

On the third day of relatively undemanding walking, the trail took us past a fine waterfall up to the ruins of Winay Wayna, where we joined the main Inca trail for the final approach to the Gateway of the Sun. I climbed the stairway with no less enthusiasm than the first time, and was rewarded with that unforgettable view of Machu Picchu. It was good to be back.

*Quechua women run rustic bars in Andean villages, making, selling and drinking copious amounts of cicha de jora, a robust and potent maize beer.*

## PERUVIAN ANDES POTATOES

*This is a version of the traditional Quechua dish known as* papa a la huancaina *that has survived the Spanish conquest, although there is an addition of black pepper introduced from India by the invaders.*

*Originally it would have been made with Peruvian yellow-fleshed potatoes but is fine with new potatoes. To give the dish its characteristic yellow colour, we have substituted turmeric for the Peruvian herb palillo, as this is more readily available. For similar reasons we suggest a yellow 'Scotch Bonnet' chilli as a substitute for the harder to find yellow aji amarillo chilli that is popular in Peru, and feta cheese as the type most similar to the Peruvian equivalent. In Peru the dish is usually served with hard-boiled egg, but we prefer it with a fried or poached egg for a lively breakfast.*

*'Scotch Bonnet' chillies are very hot and need to be treated with care. Wash your hands thoroughly after chopping and keep them away from eyes and sensitive skin.*

SERVES 4–6

1kg/2lb new potatoes, peeled and boiled until soft
200g/7oz feta cheese
250ml/9fl oz milk
4 tablespoons olive oil
1 yellow 'Scotch Bonnet' chilli, finely chopped
4 garlic cloves, finely chopped

1kg/2lb onions, thinly sliced
1/2 teaspoon ground black pepper
1/2 teaspoon turmeric
150g/5oz sweetcorn kernels
salt to taste

1 egg per person, fried or poached
about 20 black olives
handful of coriander leaves, chopped

Slice the boiled potatoes into 1/2cm/1/4in thick slices. In a blender, combine the feta cheese and the milk until smooth. Heat the oil in a large frying pan and gently fry the chilli, garlic and onion until soft and golden brown. Add the black pepper and turmeric, fry for 1 minute, lay the sliced potatoes on top and then add the corn. Pour the milk and cheese into the pan. Gently simmer until the sauce has reduced. Add salt to taste if necessary (remembering how salty feta cheese is).

Serve topped with an egg, black olives and a garnish of coriander leaves.

*Peruvian Andes potatoes*

# grenada

The significance of nutmeg to Grenada is obvious to visitors. The nut appears on the nation's flag and Grenada refers to itself as 'the Spice Island of the Caribbean' at every opportunity. Even our hotel was called the Spice Island Inn and its welcome drink was a fruit punch generously laced with fresh grated nutmeg.

The island's capital, St George's, claims to be the prettiest harbour in the Caribbean. This may be true. The curving hillside around the port, once the bowl of a volcano, is a mosaic of ochre-tiled and red-tin-roofed houses punctuated by towering churches and tropical trees. The laid-back life in the labyrinth of lanes that link the harbour to the market squares provides a seductive atmosphere for unhurried exploration. We ate lunch at a café called Deyna's, squeezed between the spice warehouses along the esplanade overlooking the Caribbean, and went straight for a Grenadian classic, the ominously named 'oil down'. This is a hearty stew of layered vegetables and fish, slow-cooked in creamy coconut milk spiced with turmeric, thyme, chives and peppers.

As we ambled through the town, the hills of St George's helped us to build up an appetite for an evening meal. In the spice market, nutmeg and mace were piled high among ginger roots, bags of ground turmeric (misleadingly referred to all over Grenada as saffron), bottles of hot sauce, necklaces of cloves and odd bundles of a bark called mauby, claimed to be a vigorous aphrodisiac. Next door in the fruit and vegetable market we saw many of the ingredients, like cashew fruit, soursop and callaloo (the green spinach-like leaves of the ubiquitous Caribbean root vegetable dasheen), that we were to eat on our gastronomic journey around the island.

The venue of our evening meal, the Nutmeg Café, gave us our chance to taste another Grenadian staple, *lambi* or curried conch. The harbour view from our first-floor window table was wonderful, as was the nutmeg-laced rum punch, the nutmeg ice cream and even the curried sauce, although conch has a difficult taste that I have yet to acquire. Later in our stay, as we drove round the island looking at the nutmeg processing plant and climbing into the rainforest of the Grand Etang hills, we saw how much Grenadians like conch when we came across mountains of empty shells piled up beside the palm-fringed beaches of white sand.

### Nutmeg and Mace
### (*Myristica fragrans*)

Nutmeg is one of the classic spices of the trade, native to just a few islands in the Banda group of the Moluccas, the Spice Islands of Indonesia. The spice is a kernel of a brown seed with an aril latticework covering which is removed to produce another spice, mace. The nutmeg part is the sweeter and more aromatic, now used in cooking, both sweet and savoury, in Europe, Arabia, the Caribbean and India as well as Indonesia. It is best used by grating a whole kernel into a dish as needed. Early use was more for its narcotic properties as a calmative drug than as a food spice.

Mace is dried in the sun to give a perfumed sweet scent that belies a bitter flavour. It is best used as whole blades grated as needed. Like nutmeg, it is used in both sweet and savoury dishes and is also used in the cosmetics industry.

*A conch shell on the west shore of Grenada.*

## GRENADIAN OIL DOWN

*This unusually named dish is a classic taste of Grenada featuring vegetables cut large and cooked slowly in coconut milk with fresh herbs and spices until very soft. Grenadians usually make the dish with salt cod or pork; here we use chunky cod. Halloumi, a salty cheese, makes a good substitute for fish if you prefer a vegetarian version of the dish: cut the halloumi into thin slices and fry them until brown on both sides in hot oil, then add in the same way as the fish.*

### SERVES 4–6

250g/9oz yam, peeled and cut into 7 x 2.5cm/3 x 1in pieces

250g/9oz pumpkin, peeled, seeded and cut as above

250g/9oz sweet potato, peeled and cut as above

115g/4oz callaloo or spinach, cut into 2.5cm/1in strips

115g/4oz kale, cut into 2.5/1in strips

1 heaped teaspoon black pepper, freshly ground

16 blades of chive, chopped

2 tablespoons flat-leaf parsley, chopped

8 sprigs of fresh thyme, roughly chopped

salt to taste

2 teaspoons turmeric

300ml/10fl oz coconut milk

350g/12oz thick cod fillet, cut into 5cm/2in strips

2 tablespoons sunflower oil

1 medium onion, finely chopped

about 24 okra, chopped

Place the yam in a medium-sized saucepan, cover well with water and bring to the boil. Add the pumpkin and sweet potato, return to the boil and gently simmer until the vegetables start to soften, then drain. In a large saucepan with a thick bottom and tight-fitting lid, layer the ingredients, starting with the callaloo and kale, followed by the yam, then another layer of the callaloo and kale, then the sweet potato, then the remaining callaloo and kale and finally the pumpkin, sprinkling each layer with the black pepper, chives, parsley, thyme and salt to taste.

Dissolve the turmeric in a tablespoon of water, then stir in another 150ml/5fl oz of water. Pour this into the oil down, along with the coconut milk. Cover the pan and as soon as it comes to the boil, reduce the heat and simmer gently for 15 minutes. Add the fish chunks and spoon the sauce over them. Replace the lid and cook for a further 10 minutes. Remove the lid and gently simmer for a further 5 minutes or until most of the liquid has been absorbed.

Serve with okra fried with onion in sunflower oil until soft.

*Grenadian oil down*

## GRENADIAN SPICED FISH

*This spice mix, which uses the ubiquitous Grenadian spice mace, is good with any fish.*

SERVES 4

4 monkfish fillets
salt to taste
12 cloves
8 whole allspice seeds
1 teaspoon mace
$^1/_2$ teaspoon turmeric

$^1/_2$ teaspoon ground black pepper
4 tablespoons olive oil
2 medium onions, thinly sliced
4 garlic cloves, finely chopped
2 teaspoons plain unbleached flour

Season the fish fillets with salt. Grind the cloves, allspice and mace to a powder and combine with the turmeric and ground black pepper. In a large frying pan, heat the oil and fry the onion with the garlic until the onion is soft and golden. Add the spice mix and fry, stirring constantly, for 1 minute, then stir in the flour. Place the fish fillets in the pan and fry them until brown on both sides. Gradually stir in 8 tablespoons of water. Cook until the sauce thickens and the fish is cooked. Add salt to taste.

## CARIBBEAN SPICED SWEET POTATOES

*This combination of mashed sweet potatoes with cinnamon, vanilla and nutmeg makes an excellent accompaniment to the main dishes in this chapter.*

SERVES 4–6

2.5cm/1in piece of cinnamon stick
$^1/_2$ teaspoon black peppercorns
3 medium-sized sweet potatoes,
  preferably with orange flesh, peeled
  and cubed
2 tablespoons milk

2 tablespoons butter
$^1/_2$ teaspoon nutmeg, freshly grated
$^1/_2$ teaspoon natural vanilla essence
grated zest of an orange
salt to taste
1 dessertspoon brown sugar

Grind the cinnamon and black pepper to a powder. Boil the sweet potatoes until soft, drain and mash with 2 tablespoons of milk and a tablespoon of butter until smooth. Stir in half of the cinnamon and pepper spice mix, plus the grated nutmeg, vanilla essence, orange zest and salt. Pile into a heatproof dish, dot with the remaining butter and sprinkle over the sugar and remaining spice mix. Cook under a pre-heated grill until the sugar and butter caramelize.

**Nets hanging up to dry on the Caribbean island of St Lucia.**

africa

Considering the vast size and geographical and climatic variety of sub-Saharan Africa, it is strange that the region is not the original home of a single spice that has been important to the spice routes. This part of the world has played a significant role, however, as a staging post.

The rapid westward expansion of Islam from Arabia took the Moors via North Africa all the way to Al Andalus (Andalucia) in southern Spain by 710. The Islamic and cultural influence of the Moors eventually spread to the nomadic desert peoples of the Sahara, the Almohads, who opened up the trans-Saharan trade routes that saw the first spices crossing the desert, establishing market towns like Marrakech.

As the Moors and Jews of Andalucia were ousted by Christians in the thirteenth century, many moved south into what is now Morocco. Some continued along the desert routes to Mali and there was a strong Islamic influence on the Songhai empire that emerged slowly over the following centuries, building up great trading cities like Walata, Tombouctou and Djenné along the River Niger. By the fourteenth century, the Malians were the Venetians of the desert, a commercial and imperial nation with well-established caravan routes north to Morocco and east to Egypt, and river connections south to West Africa's tropical coast. The caravan routes saw up to twelve thousand camels a year, which left laden with the gold and salt that were the basis of Songhai wealth, and returned with cargoes of textiles, spices, glass and ceramics. Traditions of cuisine that had begun to excite the peoples of West Africa were developed further as new food-stuffs and spices began to arrive with European traders who set up trade along the coast. West Africa probably still offers a more interesting and spicy choice of cuisine than any other part of sub-Saharan Africa.

East Africa made a significant early mark on the spice trade. Spices from across the Indian Ocean are known to have arrived in this region in ancient Egyptian times, and it became an important part of the spice routes in the late twelfth century, when Ethiopia began trading with Arab and Swahili merchants along the coast of East Africa. The complexity of the traditional Ethiopian spice mixture *berbere* is testament to the extent of this and subsequent trade: the cardamom, pepper, ajwain and ginger came from India, the nutmeg and cloves from Indonesia, the fennel, cumin and coriander from the eastern Mediterranean, and the chilli and allspice from the Americas. The development of trade was cut short by the arrival of the Portuguese in the sixteenth century. Having made their way around the Cape of Good Hope and into the Indian Ocean, the Portuguese

**LEFT:** *The River Niger was the lifeline for traders and spice merchants supplying the Songhai cities of Tombouctou and Djenné. River steamers remain one of the main forms of transport in the region.*

**PAGES 144–5:** *A cliff of Saharan sand meets the River Niger as it meanders through the deserts of Mali and Niger. The river begins its life in the rainforests of Guinea and flows north and east for thousands of miles before finding its way south again to enter the Bight of Benin from the deltas of Nigeria.*

established useful ports all around the coast of Africa. In Angola they built São Paulo de Luanda, the first European city south of the Sahara, and they fortified many of the other ports, such as El Jadida and Essaouira in Morocco, Elmina in Ghana, Fort Jesus at Mombasa and St Sebastian in Mozambique. The forts became safe ports of call for their cargo ships stopping off on their way to and from the Indies as well as convenient bases for local trade. To all these parts of Africa they imported spices and foodstuffs from Asia and then from their conquests in South America and the Caribbean.

By the end of the seventeenth century the nature of European trade with Africa had taken on a grim new face. Slaves replaced gold and ivory as the most valuable export. The effect of huge new populations of West Africans being forcibly resettled in the Americas can be seen in the dishes of Bahia in Brazil, the creole food of the Caribbean and the Cajun recipes of the southern United States.

The new products that the Portuguese imported from the Americas and Asia changed eating habits in Africa for ever. In Morocco people already used to a wide variety of eastern spices quickly incorporated the various types of chilli pepper (known in Africa as *piri piri*) and paprika into their cuisine to create recipes for harissa paste and *ras el hanout* spice mixtures. In Ghana, local peppers like melegueta, selim and Ashanti were soon swept aside in preference for imported chilli and cayenne, and local groundnuts such as hausa and bamberra were replaced by peanuts. Along with tomatoes, maize, corn, sweet potatoes, potatoes, cassava, manioc and sweet peppers, these foods are now so widely eaten all over Africa it is hard to imagine what people ate before their arrival.

The Indian Goans who followed the Portuguese to Mozambique developed a simple recipe for mixing chilli peppers with lime juice, garlic and oil to manufacture a paste still found in shops from Angola to Zimbabwe. Later, people from other parts of India settled in parts of Africa associated with Britain, including Uganda, Kenya and South Africa, taking their traditions of spicy cookery with them. However, there has been little integration of these traditions into East African cookery, which generally avoids the use of complex spice mixtures.

*This weekly market at Djenné in Mali is typical of the country markets that are the main source of spices, vegetables, fruits and household items for most villagers in rural Africa.*

# morocco

The gate man of our friend's home was a dead ringer for Obi-Wan Kenobi. The fashion for monk-like hooded cloaks (*jellabas*) among the men of coastal Morocco gives many places the look of a Jedi Knight convention on a *Star Wars* film set. Up in the High Atlas Mountains, where cold air blows off permanent snow, it makes sense to wrap up in heavy robes with a hood pulled over your face. Down on the sunny beaches of the coast it may seem less appropriate but Morocco is actually a cold country for much of the year, albeit with a hot sun. When a stiff, moist wind pounds the shore, whipping the Atlantic into angry waves and cooling the air, anyone exposed or caught in the shadows is grateful for a warm hood. We did find luxurious Mediterranean warmth, out of the wind when the sun shone. But sunbathing is not a passion of the Jedi.

We were visiting friends in Oualidia, an Atlantic resort between the ports of Safi and El Jadida. The coastline is rich agricultural land. Where other cultures might have established beach hotels, here there are miles of intensive market gardens right next to the beach. It is also a coast of ancient ports. Essaouira, Casablanca and Rabat, like Safi and El Jadida, have long histories of thriving trade stretching back thousands of years. Although the first spices were probably imported into the Magreb by Phoenecian and Roman traders centuries before Christ, it was through the mobility of Muslim Arabs migrating westwards during the seventh century and their enthusiasm for spices that many recipes using spice mixtures were first transported to Morocco. A tradition of sweet and sour flavours developed, mixing meat and fish with fruits such as dates, preserved lemons, olives and apricots and nuts like almonds and walnuts. The Atlantic ports provided opportunities for a steady supply of spices from the Arab sphere of influence and later brought by the Portuguese from across the Atlantic. Chilli and paprika were added to the flavours of Moroccan tajines, couscous sauces, basting pastes and spice mixtures.

Our friends were learning the art of rod and line fishing in the ocean from the sons of a local shopkeeper. Occasionally these two drive south

*The port of Essaouira on Morocco's Atlantic coast, fortified by the Portuguese in the seventeenth century, attracted merchants from all over the Islamic world and significant communities of Jewish traders.*

to where the Sahara meets the sea for a weekend of what they describe as 'fishing in the desert'. Some local men make a living out of line fishing the Atlantic. Fish are still plentiful enough and large enough to sell for a good price to roadside fishmongers in vans on their way to the international markets in Safi and El Jadida. On our arrival we were met by the biggest sea bass I have ever seen, freshly cleaned on the kitchen table. We wanted to try out a recipe we had been given in Essaouira for fish tajine, but first we had to go out and buy a tajine, a round, shallow bowl with a tall conical lid, fired in a clay oven. This was no problem as we had arrived on the day of Oualidia's Saturday souk.

*The brightly painted doors of a storeroom in the souk at Essaouira.*

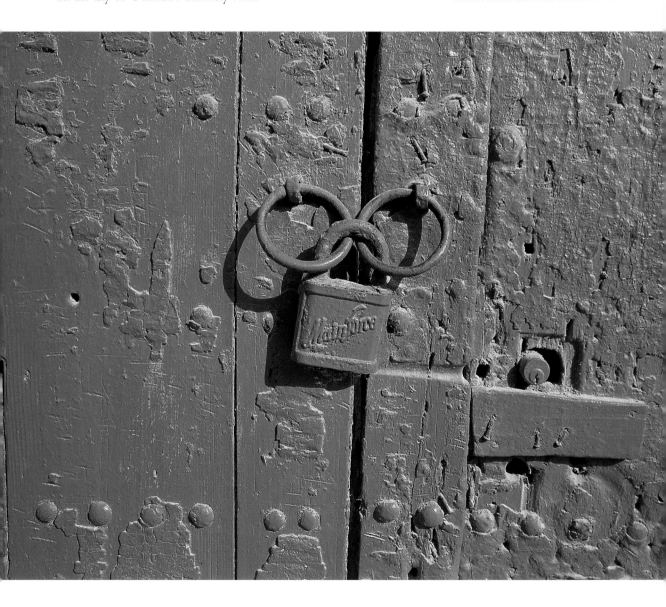

**Melegueta Pepper**
*(Afromomum melegueta)*
Melegueta pepper sometimes known as 'grains of paradise', is the one spice in all Africa that has been traded on any scale commercially on the spice routes. Even this was a relatively short-lived affair. These aromatic and pungent brownish seeds of a herbaceous plant of the ginger family, are native to West Africa. The earliest trade in them was on the routes across the Sahara, and they are still used in Morocco. For about five hundred years in the middle of the second millennium AD, melegueta was a popular spice in Europe, especially France. Since the eighteenth century its use has declined to a negligible scale outside its homeland.

This was our first experience of a rural souk at which we were the only foreigners. Recent rain had turned the well-trodden earth between stalls into a muddy soup, and violent bursts of wind played havoc with plastic sheeting. There were plenty of tajines to choose between, all costing so little that we soon found ourselves buying silver tea pots, painted tea glasses and bundles of fresh mint too. There was even a wizened water seller with a bagpipe-style water carrier, copper cups and pompom hat. I had imagined that the famous water sellers of the Jema al-Fna, the main square of the Medina in Marrakech, dressed like this to attract a fee from tourist photographers. Apparently not.

There were plenty of spices on sale from grubby sacks displayed in between piles of oversized grey underwear, Manchester United football shirts, makeshift barber's stalls and the grisly displays of dismembered animals. We had already gathered the spices we needed from the souk in Essaouira, where they are moulded into colourful pyramids of pre-mixed harissa, chermoula, *ras el hanout* combinations. We asked the man whose stall attracted us most to mix a chermoula while we watched. He happily obliged and went on to tell us in detail how to cook his favourite style of fish tajine.

Traditionally women undertake the cooking in Moroccan homes and as they rarely leave the family home to work as cooks in restaurants or cafes, and public restaurants hardly ever provide dishes as good as the home-cooked equivalent. An exception to this are the food stalls of the night market in the Jema al-Fna, in Marrakech. Here the atmosphere alone is intoxicating, and by choosing carefully from the dozens of displays offered by theatrical, animated chefs, you can get together a reasonable meal for very little cost. The equivalent experience in Essaouira is offered on the sea wall outside the fish souk next to the busy fishing harbour. A row of enthusiastic cooks display racks of freshly caught sardines, mackerel, sea bass, tuna, sole, bream, crabs, and prawns, all waiting to be barbecued on glowing braziers and served under the shade of a giant umbrella with tomato salad and freshly squeezed orange juice.

Another way to find good Moroccan cuisine is to stay in one of the old riad houses of Marrakech where family cooks cater for guests. In one of these we ate a delicious vegetable and chickpea tajine using a version of *ras el hanout* with flower petals. *Ras el hanout* is the Moroccan equivalent to garam masala in India, and every good cook has her own version combining several ingredients in varying quantities. The one on page 159 is simple but successful and also works well with lamb.

## CHERMOULA

*This chermoula is a wet spice mix for fish. Everyone has their own combination but it always includes cumin, paprika and coriander. Chermoulas can be made in advance and stored in the fridge in an airtight container. This recipe yields the right quantity for the fish tajine recipe on page 157.*

1 dessertspoon cumin seeds
1 dessertspoon coriander seeds
large pinch of saffron
1 dessertspoon ground paprika
1 teaspoon ground ginger

1/2 teaspoon cayenne pepper
handful of coriander leaves, chopped
2 garlic cloves, roughly chopped
2 tablespoons olive oil
1 teaspoon salt

In a small frying pan gently dry-roast the cumin and coriander seeds until they become aromatic. Remove them from the heat and grind to a powder. Place this powder together with all the other ingredients in a food processor and blend until they form a wet paste.

## PRESERVED LEMONS

*Preserved lemons are an important ingredient of Moroccan cooking, adding a unique taste to tajines. They are easy to make and keep for months in an airtight preserving jar. Blanched lemon quarters are a simple substitute.*

6 lemons, cut into quarters
90g/3oz sea salt
2 cinnamon sticks
1 teaspoon black peppercorns

1 teaspoon whole cloves
1 teaspoon coriander seeds
freshly squeezed lemon juice

Place a layer of lemons in the bottom of a preserving jar and sprinkle with sea salt. Repeat this process until the lemons and salt have all been used. Gently crush the lemons with the end of a rolling pin to release the juices. Add the spices and pour over enough lemon juice to cover the mixture. Cover with an airtight lid and store in a cupboard. The lemons will be ready in two weeks.

*In the tanners' pits in Fès, life has changed little since the time when Fès was an imperial city at the heart of Morocco.*

## SAFI FISH TAJINE

*If you do not own a tajine, use a large deep frying pan or a large casserole with a fitted lid.*

SERVES 4

2 450g/1lb whole sea bass, cleaned and scaled
chermoula (see page 154)
4 tablespoons olive oil
1 large red onion, cut into thin semicircles
225g/8oz celery sticks, cut lengthways then halved
225g/8oz potatoes, peeled and finely sliced

salt and pepper to taste
2 plum tomatoes, sliced
handful of flat-leaf parsley, chopped
1 teaspoon black pepper
juice of a lemon
about 20 green olives
6 preserved lemon quarters (see page 154) or 2 fresh lemons, quartered and blanched

With a sharp knife, cut both of the sides of the fish in a criss cross pattern. Rub a third of the chermoula over them, and allow them to marinade for 1 hour.

In a large tajine, or similar, heat the oil. Fry the onions until they caramelize. Add half the remaining chermoula, stir well and fry for 1 minute. Evenly distribute across the bottom of the pan. Now layer the remaining vegetables. Start with the celery sticks, laying them in a criss cross pattern on top of the onions, cover the celery with the potato, sprinkle with salt and black pepper, then cover the potato with the tomato, and sprinkle with the parsley, pepper and lemon juice

Dissolve the remaining chermoula in 125ml/4fl oz of water and pour over the vegetables. Add the olives and preserved lemons. Increase the heat and bring to the boil. Reduce the heat and cover the tajine with the lid. Gently simmer for 20 minutes, remove the lid and lay the fish on top of the vegetables. Spoon over some of the juice, replace the lid and gently cook for 25 minutes, turning the fish half way through and again spooning over the juice.

Serve immediately with crusty baguette and salad.

*Safi fish tajine*

## RAS EL HANOUT

*This recipe yields the right quantity for the vegetable tajine recipe that follows.*

2.5cm/1in piece of cinnamon stick
1 teaspoon cumin seeds
1 teaspoon coriander seeds
1/2 teaspoon black peppercorns
1/2 teaspoon cloves
1/2 teaspoon cardamom seeds (from green cardamom pods)

large pinch of saffron
1 teaspoon ground ginger
1/2 teaspoon cayenne pepper
1/3 teaspoon freshly grated nutmeg
1 teaspoon dried thyme
1 teaspoon rose petals or 1 teaspoon rose water

In a small frying pan, dry-roast the cinnamon stick, cumin seeds, coriander seeds, peppercorns, cloves and cardamom seeds until they become aromatic. Grind to a powder and combine with the remaining ingredients.

**ABOVE:** *At Zagora in the Draa Valley, modern civilization peters out: the only way forward is along the old caravan routes that link Morocco with Mali.*

## VEGETABLE AND CHICKPEA TAJINE

*A deep frying pan or casserole with a fitted lid can be used instead of a tajine. The vegetables are cut large and cooked slowly to caramelize the sauce.*

SERVES 4–6

6 tablespoons olive oil
1 red onion, cut into thin semicircles
4 garlic cloves, finely chopped
*ras el hanout* (see above)
3 carrots, cut into quarters lengthwise
2 red peppers, cut into 2.5cm/1in strips
350g/12oz pumpkin, peeled, seeded and cut into large chunks
350g/12oz sweet potatoes, cut into large chunks

350g/12oz marrow, peeled, seeded and cut into 7cm/3in chunks
2 dessertspoons tomato purée
225g/8oz cooked chickpeas
about 28 dried hunza apricots
large pinch of saffron
large handful of coriander leaves, chopped
salt to taste

**OPPOSITE:** *Ancient casbahs are dotted along the Draa Valley like sentinels. They were built to control the trade caravans supplying Marrakech, west of the Atlas Mountains, with produce from across the deserts to the east.*

In a large tajine or similar, heat the olive oil and gently fry the onion until it caramelizes. Add the garlic, fry for 1 minute, and stir in the *ras el hanout* Add the carrots and peppers and fry for a couple of minutes, stirring well. Then add the pumpkin, sweet potato and marrow. Fry for 3 minutes, stirring. Add the tomato purée, chickpeas and hunza apricots and coat all the ingredients with the spices. Add 275ml/10fl oz of water, the saffron and coriander and salt to taste. Bring to the boil, cover the pan and simmer gently until the vegetables are soft and the sauce reduces. This should take about 30 minutes.

Serve with harissa cabbage and sultana and onion chutney (see page 161) and steamed couscous.

## HARISSA

Makes 150ml/5fl oz

about 20 dried red chillies
1 ½ tablespoons cumin seeds
2 tablespoons coriander seeds

5 garlic cloves, roughly chopped
1 teaspoon sea salt
6 tablespoons olive oil

Soak the chillies in boiling water for half an hour. Meanwhile dry-roast the cumin and coriander in a small frying pan until aromatic. Remove from the heat and grind to a powder. Place all the ingredients in a food processor and blend until a thickish paste forms. Scoop into a jar and pour a little olive oil over the surface to form a seal.

Store in a fridge in an airtight container and serve with salads or couscous or to spice up cooked Moroccan meat, fish and vegetable dishes. Harissa is a strongly spiced condiment, so use with caution.

*A stall in the spice souk at Essaouira.*

## RED CABBAGE WITH HARISSA AND CORIANDER

SERVES 4–6

450g/1lb red cabbage cut into
  2.5cm/1in squares
4 tablespoons olive oil
1 large red onion, chopped
4 garlic cloves, finely chopped
2 teaspoons ground paprika

2 heaped teaspoons harissa (see left)
1½ tablespoons tomato purée
2 teaspoons honey
1 teaspoon ground black pepper
handful of coriander leaves, chopped
salt to taste

In a medium saucepan, cook the cabbage in salted boiling water until it starts to wilt but remains crunchy. Remove from the heat and immediately drain. Splash with cold water. In a large frying pan, heat the olive oil. Fry the onion until it caramelizes. Add the garlic and fry for 1 minute. Add the paprika and stir well. Add the harissa, adjusting according to taste, and fry for 1 minute, stirring well. Add the tomato purée, honey and black pepper and stir well. Add the cabbage, and stir until it is well coated. Finally add the coriander and salt to taste.

## SULTANA AND ONION CHUTNEY

90g/3oz sultanas
60g/2oz butter
1 tablespoon olive oil
3 large Spanish onions, cut into thin
  semicircles
2 garlic cloves, finely chopped

1 teaspoon ground turmeric
1 teaspoon ground cinnamon
1 teaspoon ground ginger
pinch of saffron
60g/2oz brown sugar

Place the sultanas in a bowl. Pour over 275ml/10fl oz of boiling water and set to one side. In a large frying pan, gently melt the butter. Add the olive oil, onion and garlic. Fry on a low heat until the onion caramelizes, stirring regularly. Stir the spices into the onions while frying for 1 minute. Add the sultanas and water. Add the brown sugar and bring to the boil. Simmer gently until the water has reduced and the mixture is the texture of chutney.

# ghana

In 1992 the Washington-based Conservation International, in partnership with government departments in Ghana, embarked on the Central Region Project. The aim of this has been to combine the attractions of Kakum National Park, a large area of tropical rainforest twenty miles inland from the Atlantic coast with those of two coastal towns, Cape Coast and Elmina. Both of these were once fortified trading posts, forming an important part of Ghana's long history of trade.

The castle at Elmina is the older of the two, built by the Portuguese in 1482 with the permission of the local chief, and with the intention of engaging in trade on an equal footing. I joined one of the guided tours to see the lavish living quarters of the European inhabitants, the first Catholic church in Africa, and the fine views along the coast and over Elmina's busy harbour: a lagoon alive with fish-laden *piroges* and animated barter over the catches. The most poignant part of the tour inevitably came when we were shown the castle's cavernous store rooms, originally built to house gold, ivory, cotton and animal hides, but converted in the seventeenth century into foul, insanitary, airless dungeons packed with slaves. By the time this change occurred, the Dutch had captured the castle, after a cannon bombardment from the hill behind it. The Dutch victory, which secured Elmina for over two hundred years, was soon followed by the construction of St Jago Fort on the hill to protect the castle from a future attacks.

Dutch merchants eventually began to set up home outside the safety of the castle walls and built themselves grand mansions, most of which have fallen into advanced states of decay. One of these, known as Dolphin House, had just been selected for renovation (though it still had the demolition order daubed on it). The multi-arched pastel façade of the old merchant house made an elegantly dilapidated backdrop to a busy colourful street market. Another interesting attraction in Elmina is the whimsically surreal *posuban* shrines scattered between the houses. Colourful life-size statues of figures as diverse as Adam and Eve, Dutch naval officers and tribal chiefs stand around in gardens and on rooftops and verandas outside these ancestral sites.

*The Atlantic Ocean provides good catches for the fishermen of Cape Coast.*

The castle at Cape Coast was built by the British in 1672, and the town eventually became the capital of their Gold Coast Colony. Like the Dutch, the British came in search of fortunes from gold and the slave trade. The enviable opulence of the Governor's quarters here is even more impressive than at Elmina and the dank, squalid conditions in the subterranean slave dungeons seem all the more appalling. But the British, for all their collusion with the powerful tribes of the area in forcibly sending millions of slaves across the ocean, can claim to have been instrumental in bringing it to an end. Trade returned to gold, spices, palm oil and timber. The British eventually purchased Elmina from the Dutch, and the town's main road is still called Liverpool Street, indicating the destiny of much of the cargo, but the atmosphere and nature of Elmina to this day is very different from that of Cape Coast, reflecting their different pasts.

## WEST AFRICAN TSIRE GROUND PEANUT AND SPICE MIX

*This recipe is typical of western Africa, blending peanuts, which are grown as a cash crop throughout the region, with spices from east and west, all of which arrived during the days when European sailing ships stopped off at trading ports along the coast. Tsire can be used in baking, in barbecues, mixed into sauces, or mixed with oil and used as a condiment. It is delicious sprinkled on hot buttered toast – like a spicy peanut butter. Like most spice mixtures tsire is best made fresh but will keep in a sealed jar for a couple of weeks.*

| | |
|---|---|
| 90g/3oz peanuts, shelled | 1 teaspoon dried flaked chillies |
| 8 cloves | 1/2 teaspoon ground ginger |
| 1/3 teaspoon allspice | 1/3 teaspoon freshly grated nutmeg |
| 4cm/1 1/2in piece of cinnamon stick | 1/2 teaspoon salt |

In a small pan, gently dry-roast the peanuts, stirring regularly. When golden brown, remove them from the pan and allow them to cool.

Now dry-roast the whole spices (the cloves, allspice and cinnamon) in the same pan until they become aromatic. Remove from the heat and grind to a powder. Place all the ingredients in a food processor and blend until the peanuts are finely chopped.

Store in an airtight container.

## CAPE COAST TSIRE BAKED FISH

*This is a traditional of style of fish eaten along the coast of Ghana, coated with tsire spice mix. It can either be baked, barbecued or fried. The quantity in the recipe given left is the correct amount to use in this recipe. It is sensational with monkfish, but less expensive fish can also be used.*

SERVES 6

6 7oz/200g monkfish fillets      *tsire* spice mix (see left)
olive oil

Pre-heat oven to 375°F/190°C/gas 5.

    Rub each side of the fish fillet with olive oil, then thickly coat both sides of each fish with the spice mix. Place on a baking tray. Drizzle with a little additional olive oil. Bake in the oven for 20 minutes.

*These painted wooden statues, which blend elements of Christianity with traditional West African lore, stand outside the posuban shrines in the port of Elmina in Ghana.*

## PIRI PIRI SAUCE

Piri piri *is a term used in parts of Africa with a Portuguese past for chillies or sauces and pastes using them. The sauce or paste is a classic product of the spice routes, introduced to Africa by Goans from India using spices from the Americas delivered by Europeans and blended with pepper from the Malabar Coast. Similar pastes in French-speaking parts of Africa are known as* pil pil. *Piri piri is very versatile: an excellent marinade for barbecues, rubbed into roast chicken or served as a condiment, it keeps well for a long time in a fridge in an airtight container so you can make lots and keep it for future use. There are variations but chillies, lemons, oil, garlic and salt are essential.*

MAKES ABOUT 300ML/10FL OZ

8 large fresh red chillies, roughly
  chopped
4 garlic cloves, roughly chopped
2 teaspoons ground paprika

1 teaspoon ground black pepper
1 teaspoon salt
100ml/3fl oz lemon juice
125ml/4fl oz olive oil

Place all the ingredients in a food processor and blend into a smooth sauce. Pour into an airtight container and store in the fridge until needed.

## BARBECUED PRAWNS WITH PIRI PIRI BARBECUED SWEETCORN AND SWEET POTATO CHIPS

*Tolerance for spicy foods varies greatly from one person to the next. So only use as much* piri piri *sauce as you think you can stand.*

SERVES 4

20 jumbo prawns
4 corn cobs, cut into thirds
450g/1lb sweet potatoes, cut
  lengthwise into large chips

*piri piri* sauce (see above), to taste
olive oil

Marinade the prawns, corn cobs and sweet potatoes in *piri piri* sauce for 1 hour. When the barbecue is ready, drizzle the ingredients with a little olive oil and place the corn and sweet potato on the barbecue. Cook until golden brown on each side, crunchy on the outside and soft in the middle. Add the prawns towards the end of the cooking as they will be ready much quicker. Cook on both sides and serve.

**Barbecued prawns with piri piri barbecued sweetcorn and sweet potato chips**

the indian ocean

Despite having no indigenous spices, some of the Indian Ocean islands have played significant roles in the history of the spice trade. Mauritius was uninhabited when tenth-century Arab traders named it Dinarobin, and still uninhabited when Portuguese sailors stopped off five hundred years later, although it was home to that now famously extinct species, the dodo. It was not until the end of the sixteenth century that the Dutch finally colonized the island, naming it Mauritius after its first governor, Maurice of Nassau. It was a convenient stopover between their main port in the Indies, Batavia (now Jakarta) on Java, and their home base of Amsterdam. In 1710, the Dutch abandoned Mauritius to pirates, also abandoning a community of slaves they had brought over from Africa. Meanwhile the French had set up camp on nearby Île Bourbon (Réunion), and within five years had decided to claim Mauritius too, renaming it Île de France. The French occupied the island and developed it as a port for the French East India Company and a producer of sugar cane. Sugar cane plantations began to take over the island, worked by hundreds of slaves brought from Africa.

In 1766 a new governor, named Pierre Poivre, was appointed to Île de France from Paris. Poivre was no stranger to the island, having visited it twenty years earlier while recovering from the amputation of his arm (blown off by a cannon ball in a naval encounter with a British frigate in 1745). He deduced that the fertile soil and tropical climate might provide France with an opportunity to grow commercial quantities of Far Eastern spices which could then be shipped to Europe, breaking the long-standing Dutch monopoly on the lucrative trade. He realized that the Dutch spent so much effort guarding every sack of nutmeg and cloves piled up for export to Europe, India, China and the Americas because they feared another nation stealing seeds to grow the spices somewhere other than the Spice Islands. Despite their domination of the trade in pepper from the Malabar and cinnamon from Ceylon (Sri Lanka), it was their monopoly of nutmeg and cloves that grew nowhere outside the Spice Islands that

**PAGES 168–9:** *Fishermen set out for the evening, as they have done for centuries, from the Indian Ocean island of Zanzibar.*

**RIGHT:** *Miles of deserted white sandy beaches and the clear warm waters of the Indian Ocean surround the islands of the Seychelles archipelago. Now a tropical paradise for tourists, the islands were occupied by the French in the eighteenth century, providing them with ideal conditions to establish spice plantations.*

*A street market in the Mauritian capital, Port Louis.*

made the Dutch position as the most powerful players in the spice trade unassailable. They had been careful to concentrate production on a few closely guarded islands: nutmeg on the Bandas and cloves on Ambon. Theft of a single shoot was punishable by death, and surplus harvests were incinerated to keep prices high.

Poivre made a series of daring expeditions from Manila into the Moluccan archipelago and in 1770 the French merchant ship *Étoile du Martin* berthed at the capital of Île de France, Port Louis, packed with smuggled plants, seeds and nuts of nutmeg, cloves and pepper. Under the watchful eye of Poivre, commercial quantities of all these spices were soon being cultivated in Île de France, and the Dutch monopoly was gone for ever. The French consolidated their rise in the trade by establishing plantations in their other tropical colonies, including Indian Ocean islands such as Île Bourbon and the Seychelles, and on the Caribbean coast of South America in Guyana. Poivre earned a place in the history of the spice trade, and has been immortalized in the tongue twister 'Peter Piper picked a peck of pickled pepper'.

This French coup was short-lived. Not long after Poivre's death in 1786, the French Revolution rid Île de France of its governor, the island became a hotbed of Indian Ocean piracy, and the French East India Company collapsed. In 1814, following the defeat of Napoleon, the British claimed Île de France and the Seychelles as spoils of war. The nutmeg and cloves that had made successive fortunes for the Portuguese, Dutch and French were now in British hands.

The British gave the island back its old name of Mauritius, exported cloves and nutmeg around their own tropical colonies, and abandoned commercial spice cultivation on Mauritius in favour of sugar and tea plantations. From 1835 onwards, slaves from Africa were replaced by indentured labourers from India and China. It is the rich mix of African, Indian, Chinese, French and British influences that makes Mauritius such an interesting island to visit in terms of both culture and cuisine.

# mauritius

When Mauritius gained independence in 1968, Indians were in a majority and many had risen socially far from their plantation past. Ethnic Indians have dominated post-colonial democratic government of the island ever since. When a temple bell rings out across the water of the crater lake at Grand Bassin, and miniature armadas of offerings, flowers, fruits and flickering candles floating on homemade rafts of dried leaves drift by, the scene could be taking place on the banks of the Ganges. Giant statues of Hindu deities stand in clouds of incense smoke and passively receive processions of chanting devotees. This is a typical Sunday on the shore of a holy lake thousands of miles from India high in the volcanic mountains of Mauritius. Few of the *puja*-engrossed men, or women in colourful saris or neatly dressed children with well-oiled hair have ever been to India. None of the apparently Indian people I spoke to saw themselves as anything other than Mauritian, their original languages having merged into a kind of Hindi called Bhojpuri.

However, Mauritius is not overwhelmingly Indian in flavour. French Creole is by far the most frequently used language. Of the Europeans on the island, the French are the most numerous. There are mosques and churches alongside Hindu temples in most towns. The Creole dance *sega*, a sort of Creole salsa, dominates cultural evenings on the island's many hotels. Hotel food is often a buffet blend of tamed Creole, classical French and rather bland international dishes. Away from the hotels, there is an abundance of good spicy Creole, Indian and Chinese food: in Mauritius street food is big business. But many of the hotels on Mauritius are such temples of hedonistic pleasures, built on beaches of fine white sand, lapped by the warm water of clear blue lagoons filled with colourful coral and exotic fish, that guests rarely leave them.

For those who do venture beyond the hotel gates, there are plenty of pleasures to be found, and Mauritius is small enough to explore in a few days with a hire car. The interior is still dominated by acres of golden sugar cane between dramatic mountains of dark, jagged volcanic rock and reservoirs surrounded by casuarina trees that make popular and tranquil picnic spots. To the south, the island is too mountainous for sugar cane. The Black River Gorges National Park is an untamed landscape of spectacular views, lush green vegetation and waterfalls. The park is another

popular picnic destination. Mauritians are big on picnics, and people are so friendly towards the relatively few tourists that we found it hard not to get involved in several large-scale picnics. On a drive through the park we saw that many of the picnicking families were busy picking berries off bushes, so we stopped to see what they were. The berries were bitter, eaten with dried chilli flakes and salt: an acquired taste!

*Mauritian cuisine blends French, Creole, Indian and Chinese influences and depends on plenty of fresh fish and seafood.*

Most of the other food we found in bustling markets and in the street cafés of villages where we stopped was easier to enjoy, and often excellent. Creole cooking is a blend of African and Indian from the days of slavery and indentured labour, together with French and a little bit of Chinese. During the twentieth century there was a large increase in the Chinese population, both from mainland China and from Hong Kong, attracted to opportunities in retail and business. The main contribution of the Chinese to street food has been flour noodles served in soups from steaming barrows. In Port Louis we ate dholl purées; pancakes with *rougaille*, a garlic and tomato sauce, and *bredes*, which are spinach-like greens. We also found plenty of typically Indian samosas and bhajias of vegetables fried in spicy batter. Our most memorable dish from the culinary melting pot of Mauritius is fish *vindaye*. The word *vindaye* has the same Portuguese origins as vindaloo, *vinho de alho* (literally, 'garlic wine'). In this case it refers to a marinade that combines garlic with mustard, green chillies, vinegar and turmeric.

## MAURITIAN VINDAYE ACHARD DES LEGUMES

MAKES 750ML/26FL OZ

115g/4oz carrots, cut into thin strips
90g/3oz fine green beans, topped and
 tailed and cut in half
150g/5oz white cabbage, cut into thin
 strips
half a green pepper, cut into thin strips
3 tablespoons sunflower oil
1 medium onion, thinly sliced

1 large garlic clove, finely chopped
1 dessertspoon turmeric
2 green chillies, thinly sliced
60ml/2fl oz cider vinegar
1 tablespoon yellow mustard seeds,
 crushed
salt to taste

*Vindaye **is a popular Mauritian side dish blending European, Asian and local traditions. It is usually served in small quantities, like a pickle. This** vindaye **is similar to piccalilli, with the addition of chillies and turmeric.***

Plunge the carrots, beans, cabbage and pepper into boiling water for 2 minutes, drain and refresh with cold water, and set to one side.

In a wok, heat the oil and fry the onion and garlic until soft. Add the turmeric and fry for 1 minute, then add 125ml/4fl oz of water and simmer for 1 minute. Take off the heat and combine the sauce with the vegetables, chilli, vinegar, mustard seeds and salt to taste. Spoon into an airtight jar, pushing the vegetables down and pouring the remaining liquid over the top. Seal the jar and leave for 24 hours before serving to allow the vegetables to soak up the yellow sauce. Store in the fridge.

Serve with the fish *rougaille* dish, opposite, or as an accompaniment to any meal.

## MAURITIAN ROUGAILLE SAUCE

*This sauce is a Mauritian speciality that combines garlic, chillies and herbs with pepper and tomatoes. It has a distinctive French and Creole flavour. It is always served piping hot and can be eaten with chicken, fish or vegetables. The recipe given here works best with fish.*

3 tablespoons sunflower oil
3 green chilli peppers, chopped
  (optional)
½ teaspoon chilli powder
2.5cm/1in piece of ginger, finely
  chopped
3 garlic cloves, finely chopped
3 red onions, thinly sliced

1 tablespoon tomato purée
handful of fresh thyme leaves
250g/9oz cherry tomatoes, pulped in
  a food processor
handful of parsley, finely chopped
½ teaspoon freshly ground black
  pepper
salt to taste

In a saucepan, heat the oil until it is very hot, then fry the chopped green chilli and chilli powder for 30 seconds; add the ginger and garlic and fry for another 30 seconds; add the onions and fry until they are golden brown.

Add the tomato purée and thyme, fry for another 30 seconds, add the pulped tomatoes, cover and simmer for 5 minutes until the sauce reduces. Then add 125ml/4fl oz water, parsley, pepper and salt and simmer for 1 minute.

## MAURITIAN ROUGAILLE FISH

*Using the recipe for* rougaille *sauce above, this Mauritian fish dish is quick and easy to prepare.*

SERVES 4

2 tablespoons sunflower oil
4 200g/7oz chunky cod fillets

salt to taste
*rougaille* sauce (see above)

In a large frying pan, heat the oil, add the fish fillets seasoned with salt, and fry until golden brown. Carefully remove from the frying pan.

In the remaining oil left in the pan, fry the *rougaille* sauce with a little water for 3 minutes. Return the fillets to the pan, spoon the sauce over them and gently cook for a further 3 minutes.

**The weekly market in the provinical
Mauritian town of Flacq.**

# the seychelles

The Seychelles had a very similar early history to that of Mauritius, and there is a similar blend of African, Asian and European influences on culture and cuisine. The Seychelles do not have the sugar cane plantations of Mauritius, but have been important islands of spice production. Cinnamon remains an economically important crop and there are still vanilla plantations. For the most part, however, the Seychelles are marketed as an idyllic tropical paradise, with miles of white sand beaches and warm tropical waters. Tourism now provides around half the nation's gross national product, and most of the spices grown there today are in people's gardens.

## SEYCHELLES FISH

*This recipe uses fillets that have been marinaded with the flavours of ginger, cinnamon and pepper, then cooked in a coconut cream and curry leaf, chilli and turmeric sauce.*

SERVES 4

4 6oz/175g red snapper fillets
salt to taste
juice of a lime
2in/5cm piece of ginger, peeled and
  grated
6 black peppercorns, crushed
1 cinnamon stick, broken up
2 tablespoons groundnut oil

2 large red onions, thinly sliced
3 garlic cloves, finely chopped
2 green chillies, cut into thin strips
10 curry leaves
1 teaspoon turmeric
400ml/14fl oz coconut milk
1 dessertspoon lime juice

Season the fish fillets with salt and marinade them in the lime juice with half the grated ginger, the peppercorns and the cinnamon stick for 30 minutes.

In a large frying pan, heat the oil. Fry the onions until they become translucent, then add the garlic, chilli, curry leaves and remaining grated ginger, and fry for 1 minute. Add the turmeric, stir in the coconut milk and 125ml/4fl oz of water, and gently simmer for 2 minutes, taking care not to boil as the coconut milk will separate. Add salt to taste, then lay the fish fillets across the bottom of the pan with any remaining marinade. Simmer gently until the fish is tender and cooked through. Remove from the heat and stir in the dessertspoon of lime juice. Serve immediately.

**ABOVE: Strange granite rock formations on the island of La Digue in the Seychelles.**

**OPPOSITE: Seychelles fish**

# zanzibar

Much closer to the African mainland than either Mauritius or the Seychelles, Zanzibar was inhabited from an earlier date. In the first century AD, the islands of Unguja (Zanzibar) and Pemba, which are the principal islands of modern Zanzibar, were part of the Kingdom of Saba' (the biblical Sheba), based in what is now Yemen in south-western Arabia. The monsoon winds made trade and travel between East Africa and Arabia an annual activity. By the tenth century, communities of Omani Arabs and Shirazi Persians had settled on Zanzibar to trade with the Kiswahili-speaking Bantu people of the mainland. Silk and porcelain from China and cotton and spices from India were being exchanged for local goods that included ivory, gold, amber and rhinoceros horn.

Following Vasco da Gama's first visit to Zanzibar during his historic voyage around Africa to India in 1497, the Portuguese took control of the islands as part of their expansion around Mombasa. They used them as a port of call between Asia and Europe until their expulsion in 1698 by the navy of the Omani Sultan. Zanzibar was then ruled from Muscat and became a valuable asset to Oman as a centre of slavery which emerged as a thriving trade. Whole communities in East Africa were devastated as the young and strong were captured and sold for export.

By the nineteenth century Oman was a major trading nation of the Indian Ocean. In 1820 Sultan Sa'id decided to develop the infant industry of clove plantations with seeds from Mauritius and the Seychelles. The vast plantations that were established on Zanzibar were so successful that by the second half of the nineteenth century Zanzibar supplied more than 90 per cent of the world's traded supply, and its trade in cloves reduced the production in the Moluccas to an insignificant local industry thousands of miles further away from the lucrative markets of the west.

The cloves were harvested by slaves and sent to Zanzibar Town to be processed into oil. The town became the opulent centre of a powerful and prosperous state. Sa'id moved his capital there from Muscat, and the island was transformed into one of the great spice islands of international trade. It attracted merchants from many parts of the world, developing a much more varied and sophisticated tradition of cookery than the mainland of East Africa only a few dozen miles away.

Zanzibar's good fortune was brief. After Sa'id's death the islands split away from Oman. Zanzibar was subsequently hit by plagues, clove prices fell, and then it was occupied by the British. The islands were eventually granted independence in 1963, and after a brief, bloody revolution, the islands of Zanzibar and Pemba joined Tanganyika on the mainland to become the modern nation of Tanzania.

Zanzibar has kept much of its unique atmosphere and romantic image. The dhow harbour, which must have been so busy in the heyday of the spice trade, is still used today and many of the grand buildings of the spice merchants are being restored. Cloves remain the most important export, but ironically most of them are shipped to Indonesia, the original home of cloves, to supply the huge demand for clove cigarettes that are a national passion there. There are many spice plantations in the interior of the island, with cloves being joined by almost every traded spice.

When I first visited Zanzibar in the 1980s the island was unused to tourism. There were only a few places to stay or eat, and foreigners were a novelty. On two occasions I was robbed by policemen. Ten years later, when I returned to photograph an offshore ecotourism project, much had changed. Zanzibar was brimming with tourists, there were *bureaux de change* and internet cafés in the old Stone Town and street lights in the alleyways. There was a plethora of smart hotels in restored and converted merchant houses and a string of holiday camps along the east coast.

My stay on the main island was brief. I crossed to Chumbe Island in a little open motor boat over a channel of the Indian Ocean busy with fishing dhows, and found myself in an isolated paradise. Until recently, the tiny island was owned by the military and nobody was allowed near it. This has left it with pristine coral reefs, undisturbed by fishermen or tourists. The project accommodates visitors in Robinson Crusoe-style ecovillas with solar panels and cleverly designed rain-collecting roofs thatched with palm leaves. With copious supplies of fresh fish, vegetables, rice, spices and beer, and a staff of rangers and cooks recruited from local villages, Chumbe offers visitors a chance to live in simple comfort and quietly indulge themselves in the peace and unspoiled natural history of the island.

The food was excellent. We had breakfast and lunch in the cool shade and ocean breeze of an open terrace. Dinner was eaten communally with other guests and staff by candlelight in the warm night air. It was like being at a great dinner party every night.

ABOVE: *The Anglican Cathedral in Zanzibar's historic Stone Town has been built on the site of the island's old slave market.*

PAGES 180–81: *Dhows are the ubiquitous sailing craft of the Indian Ocean, and have been since the beginning of the spice trade. Around the island of Zanzibar and along the Swahili coast of East Africa, they are still in everyday use.*

## ZANZIBAR CURRY POWDER

*This recipe was shown to me by Khadije, the resident cook on Chumbe Island at the time of my visit. We use this in the Zanzibar egg curry on page 185. It is also used with vegetable dishes.*

| | |
|---|---|
| 1 dessertspoon coriander seeds | ½ teaspoon turmeric |
| 1 teaspoon cumin seeds | 1 teaspoon red chilli powder |
| 1 dessertspoon mustard seeds | 1 teaspoon paprika |
| 1 teaspoon fennel seeds | 5cm/2in piece jaggery or 1 tablespoon |
| ½ teaspoon fenugreek seeds | brown sugar |
| 2.5cm/1in piece cinnamon stick | |

In a small frying pan, dry-roast all the seeds and the cinnamon stick until aromatic. Remove from pan and grind to a powder. Combine with the remaining spices and the jaggery.

*A mosque on the Arabian Sea coast of Oman dating from the nineteenth century, when the Omani Sultan Sa'id established the first clove plantations on Zanzibar, using seeds collected from Mauritius and the Seychelles.*

*Khadije, one of the cooks on Chumbe Island, provides excellent home cooking for guests staying in the island's ecovillas.*

## ZANZIBAR EGG CURRY

SERVES 4–6

9 eggs
4 medium red onions, roughly chopped
2.5cm/1in piece of fresh ginger, peeled and roughly chopped
2 garlic cloves, roughly chopped
2 red chillies

4 large tomatoes, roughly chopped
Zanzibar curry powder (see page 183)
4 tablespoons sunflower oil
225g/8oz podded fresh peas
salt to taste
handful of coriander leaves, chopped

Boil the eggs until hard-boiled, remove from pan and immerse in cold water, to prevent the yolk blackening. When cool, peel and cut in half and set to one side.

In a blender, pulp the onions, ginger, garlic and chilli until smooth and remove from blender. Blend the tomatoes and Zanzibar curry powder until smooth. In a large wok, heat the oil, and when hot add the onion mixture and fry for 2 minutes. Add the blended tomato and spice mix and 1 cup of water. Bring to the boil, reduce heat and simmer gently until the oil returns and the sauce is reduced. Add the peas, eggs and salt to taste, and simmer for a further 5 minutes.

Garnish with fresh coriander and serve with rice or fried potatoes.

## ZANZIBAR FISH CURRY MASALA

*This is a spice mixture I was shown on Chumbe Island to use in fish dishes. The cardamom and lemon grass flavours make it quite different from the spice mixture used above for vegetable and egg dishes. Here we use it in a delicious prawn curry.*

1 teaspoon cumin seeds
1 dessertspoon coriander seeds
1 teaspoon black peppercorns
8 green cardamom pods, shelled
2.5cm/1in piece of cinnamon stick

1 teaspoon dried lemon grass powder
1 teaspoon ground ginger
1 teaspoon turmeric
1 teaspoon paprika

In a small frying pan, dry-roast the cumin, coriander, peppercorns, cardamom seeds and cinnamon stick until aromatic. Remove from the pan and grind to a powder. Combine with the remaining ingredients.

## ZANZIBAR MASALA PRAWNS

SERVES 4

Zanzibar fish masala (see page 185)
2 red onions, roughly chopped
1 tablespoon vinegar
1 tablespoon lime juice
2 green chillies
400g/14oz uncooked prawns

4 tablespoons sunflower oil
2 red onions, thinly sliced
3 large tomatoes, cut into small cubes
salt to taste
handful of coriander leaves, chopped

Take half the Zanzibar fish masala and blend in a processor with the onions, vinegar, lime juice and green chillies until a paste forms. Cover the prawns with the paste and leave to marinade for 30 minutes.

In a large frying pan, heat 2 tablespoons of sunflower oil. Add the prawns with the marinade and fry until they are cooked through. Remove from the wok, add another 2 tablespoons of sunflower oil and fry the sliced red onions until they start to brown. Add the remaining Zanzibar fish masala and fry for 30 seconds, stirring regularly. Add the tomatoes and fry for 3 minutes, then add 150ml/5fl oz water and salt to taste, and simmer until the oil returns and the sauce reduces. Return the prawns to the wok and simmer for a further 3 minutes.

Garnish with the coriander leaves and serve with buttered rice, below.

## BUTTERED RICE

*This recipe for buttered rice brings together some of the main spices grown on Zanzibar, making the rice aromatic and flavoursome. It goes well with any of the dishes described in this chapter.*

SERVES 6

2 tablespoons butter
1 dessertspoon cumin seeds
1 cinnamon stick, broken up

8 green cardamom pods, shelled
8 cloves
425g/15oz basmati rice, washed

In a medium saucepan, melt the butter, add the spices and fry for 30 seconds. Add the washed rice, and stir to coat the rice with the butter. Add enough cold water to cover the rice by 1cm/½in. Cover with a lid and bring to the boil. Reduce heat to a minimum and cook gently until all the water has been absorbed.

*Zanzibar masala prawns*

# index

Recipes are indexed in **bold type**, *illustrations in italic*.
An asterisk* indicates detailed information about a particular ingredient.

COMMISSIONING EDITOR *Jo Christian*
SENIOR ART EDITOR *Jo Grey*
PROJECT EDITOR *Michael Brunström*
ART EDITOR *Louise Kirby*
FOOD STYLING *Nicola Fowler*
ARTWORK *Tim Vyner*
EDITORIAL ASSISTANCE *Serena Dilnot and Sarah Mitchell*
HISTORICAL CONSULTANT *Jon Wilson*
INDEXER *Roger Owen*
PRODUCTION *Kim Oliver*

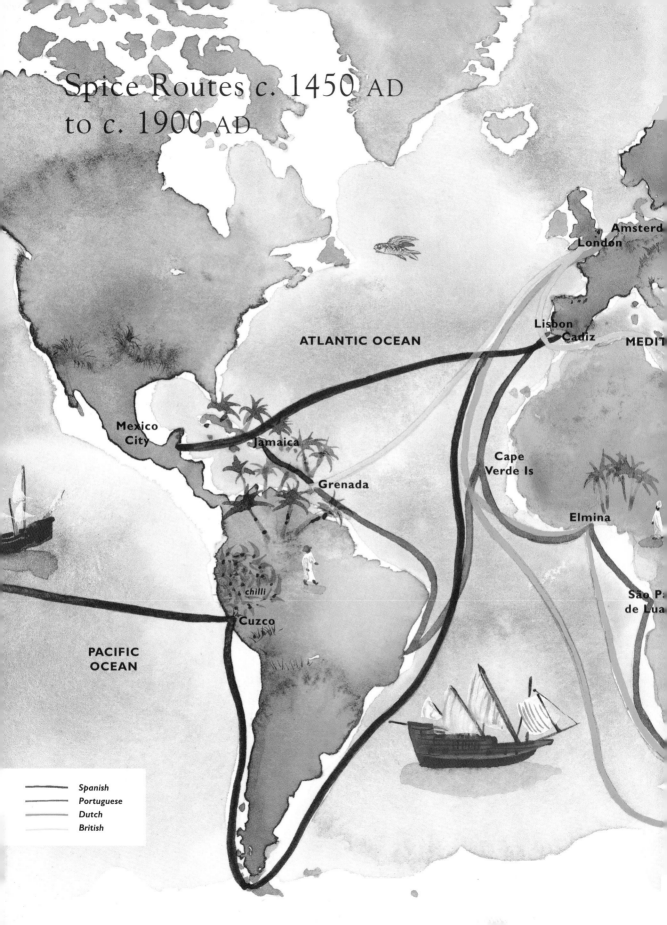

# Spice Routes c. 1450 AD to c. 1900 AD

ATLANTIC OCEAN

Amsterd
London

Lisbon
Cadiz

MEDIT

Mexico
City

Jamaica

Grenada

Cape
Verde Is

Elmina

chilli

São P.
de Lua

Cuzco

PACIFIC
OCEAN

Spanish
Portuguese
Dutch
British